PARALLEL

WORLDS

PAUL GODRICH

Ark House Press
arkhousepress.com

© 2025 PAUL GODRICH

All rights reserved. Apart from any fair dealing for the purpose of study, research, criticism, or review, as permitted under the Copyright Act, no part may be reproduced by any process without written permission.

This is a work of fiction. Unless otherwise indicated, all the names, characters, businesses, places, events and incidents in this book are either the product of the author's imagination or used in a fictitious manner. Any resemblance to actual persons, living or dead, or actual events is purely coincidental.

Cataloguing in Publication Data:
Title: Parallel Worlds
ISBN: 978-0-6459673-5-7 (pbk)
Subjects: Fiction

Design by initiateagency.com

*To my beautiful wife, Sasha.
You are God's gift to me.*

PREFACE

I once had a dream that revealed the unfolding of three distinct, yet related worlds, like layers on a cake, a three-part drama occurring simultaneously, unveiling the parallel worlds of man. The first world is that surface or outer world, our relational or social world of family, school, work, recreation etc; this is our world made visible, that which everyone thinks is everything. Then there is a deeper world, somewhat hidden yet more significant, the inner psychological world, that is affected by our exterior life but which has, in fact, the greater inclination to influence the external. To name it as our personality would go too far, for that we need to go deeper into a third world, an interior existence which throughout the personality's history has often been overwhelmed by the ego, nonetheless, this deepest life is more powerful than the ego, in fact the ego owes its very existence to this third world, not as a direct creation or manifestation of the deeper life but as a product of its absence, or negation, or abdication. This third world is at the core of our existence, and is undoubtedly spiritual. A child growing up in a home without a mother or father possesses indeterminable knowledge of what their life could, or should be like, or how their personality would have developed were they to have enjoyed living with both parents. In similar fashion, suspended over every individual's existence like Damocles' sword is an intense "What if?" an enduring "Could have been!" due directly to the absence of Life in that core world. These questions manifest themselves in every aspect of man's existence, and the level to which they are answered determines the strength of our identity in the second (psychological) and first (behavioural) worlds. When the epicentre of our being is awakened, it changes us from the inside out, affecting first our personal psychology, which simultaneously influences our behaviour and sociology.

The conclusion of my dream brought with it the conviction to write about its essence. This story, *Parallel Worlds: The Man With No Name*, is inspired by the dream. In it I set out to explore in story-form the interaction and interrelation of the three worlds of man: social, psychological, and spiritual. That was my intent. However, upon engaging the task, the story developed a life of its own. No longer can it be defined simply as allegory (as originally expected), rather, it has become an adventure, a tale explored and enjoyed for its own sake. Instead of being conditioned and confined within a singular layer of meaning, it can now be received, and applied, according to the state of the reader.

It is what I like to call a true story, in a similar way that many fairy tales are true stories. The fairy tale can be enjoyed in and of itself. However, if the reader is of a certain mind and heart, it does more than merely entertain through adventure and fantasy; it may be entertaining and fantastic but it also encapsulates and elaborates truth. Our world would be a barren and ignorant place without the enlightenment Rapunzel brings concerning the truth that beauty, as well as ugliness, is in the heart and not the eye of the beholder. Likewise, were it not for Beauty and The Beast, most would not have a clue that love has the magical power to return man from the animal state to the human. Snow White reveals two kinds of beauty, one of which is its own paradox, an ugly beauty, a cold cruel vanity, that invariably seeks to destroy the truly beautiful, versus that pure and innocent beauty, which is becoming more difficult to locate in our world, but can still be found among children in every society. In the end, as with all true stories, evil, along with its insidious ugliness, brings about its own demise, leaving the truly beautiful to live happily ever after. In like fashion, Parallel Worlds: The Man with No Name, reveals truth in its most palatable form, as a story.

*Wheels are turning
Three there are
ever near
the wandering star
sleep to wake
bound to be free
relative to the One
Coalesced Reality
Co-responding worlds
wherein we play our part
great or small
depending upon the whether
we live in all
or just a measure*

CHAPTER 1

A Rude Awakening

Dreams faded, as consciousness penetrated the outer stratums of Brosnan's being. His eyelids flickered once or twice and then opened to a blur of purple, strands of worn and fading carpet; eventually focusing on the aged mahogany base of the library directly before him. His gaze rose slowly, passing one shelf of literary treasure after another, then glided higher to where the clock, an old chimer that performed its solitary task to perfection, let him know many hours had transpired. Brosnan brought his most recent memory to the fore: He had risen from the chair to the sound of the old girl's 10 o-clock anthem, intent on visiting the bathroom, before finally retiring to his wife's side. Then, nothing! Now the clock was on the wrong side of 3am, its pendulum swaying mesmerically, and Brosnan realised he had been lying unconscious on the floor of his study for over five hours.

Two years prior, an awakening such as this would have been disturbing, to say the least; but Brosnan had grown somewhat accustomed to these catatonic intrusions. In uncharacteristic moments of light-hearted reflection, he persuaded himself they were unpredictable anomalies, some kind of psychological compensation for an overly mundane life, as perhaps occurs when a man finds himself hallucinating during a sensory-deprevation experimentation. He also congratulated himself that as yet, his unconscious experiences lay undiscovered. On a singular occasion he awoke at the foot of his library, his head cradled in Evelyn's lap, her hand wiping blood from his forehead, anxiety glaring through dark brown glassy eyes, her voice tensely straining comfort through inquiry. He dispelled the misfit rather convincingly, he thought, "I err, I must have fallen whilst resetting the old girl's time," he stammered. "I was on the third shelf and somehow lost balance."

There was also the time when Evelyn tried, in vain, to wake him from the anomalous state while Brosnan remained slumped over his desk. He shuddered his way into consciousness after ten or so minutes, and, in attempted reassurance, said he had taken a sleeping tablet with a glass of wine.

This early morning arousal, however, with the open fire reduced to a faint glow of tiny embers and winter's chill air snaking through the house, was not the moment for light-hearted jest. Rather it aroused Brosnan's deep sense of isolation and self-doubt. He picked himself up from the floor and carried his uncertainty upstairs.

CHAPTER 2

A Season Out of Place

There was something irregular about that study. Everyone, Evelyn above all, tried to convince Brosnan to get a life outside his books although recent endeavours to expand his horizons of interest seemed futile. His study had gained magnetic attraction and it became increasingly difficult to pry him away from the desk. He would, should Evelyn allow, eat drink and sleep there.

Meeting by chance while attending university, Brosnan, a 4th year undergrad, found Evelyn irresistible: vibrant, funny, passionate, creative; and totally disarming. Brosnan was a bookman, hardly the romantic; *cogito ergo sum* signified his whole approach to life. Nevertheless, Evelyn conjured a flame and the fire never faded; developing over the years into a deep wave of love that spanned their ocean, enveloping and determining every season of life in its misty perfection.

However, this season was unusual; there was no discernible rhythm: for the laws of their romance lay neglected. Brosnan's preoccupations bore down upon Evelyn and she was left feeling untouched of late. His occasional welcome embrace feathered across the surface of her body, but each stroke lacked its necessary commitment, and affection's arrow missed penetrating the mark of her soul. Attention to romance fell like autumn leaves, overshadowed by an intensifying storm of ideas and formulae that blew through their days and rained on their nights; an ever-present conceptual thorn in Evelyn's side; a thorn she tried to bear with few complaints.

Brosnan's late-night scribing of figures, beyond her interest but not her intellect, challenged Evelyn's enchantment. Her natural optimism and romantic musings kept her near the truth for which he was searching. Brosnan wasn't oblivious to Evelyn's growing pain and perplexity. He enjoyed her delights but found no time to toy and trivialise. His attention was elsewhere, and he lacked the eyes to see in her love the passion commensurate with his own earnest pulse. He could not afford the diversion; He was onto something *Substantial!* The nature of his search deliberately required romantic evasion, at least for now; until he found what he was looking for.

Brosnan did, however, consider that a reoccurring dream, a dream that had him gasping for air, such that occasionally Evelyn would rouse to his respiratory struggle, and in turn wake him, might shine some insight upon the growing estrangement between them. The details of the dream he did not care to share, except to say that in it he felt as though he were drowning.

CHAPTER

The Self-Invited Guest

Brosnan's quest intensified shortly after attending a dinner party held by Evelyn's cousin, Ramose: A rather dreary occasion, full of the kind of people who try to impress by association.

Evelyn possessed enough flair and grace to ignore the pomp and circumstance, but believed a party is never impressive unless it is expressive; When everyone is trying similarly to impress one another it falls in on itself and misses the point. "The point being, my dearest," as Evelyn would always delight in telling Brosnan, "is to *enjoy* the party."

She was determined to boost the occasion and flaunted with the seams of protocol, infusing as much energy and gaiety into as many guests as possible: The Haiges, the Forsythes, and the Ponsinghams, even dour Reverend Ramshorn, were all disarmed by her charm and for a moment their monotonous charade was interrupted as they forgot themselves in laughter.

Brosnan always admired Evelyn's facility in that regard. Possessing no appreciation or tolerance for pretence, Brosnan's attending of the event was solely to please his wife. He wanted nothing from the evening except to be engaged in as little meaningless conversation as possible.

Spying Ramose heading in his direction brought a visceral search for escape. Ramose was one who thought himself to be somebody; who thought others existed to help him be that somebody; who could sneer but never laugh; who gave quick and shifty glances; who was happy to speak but unhappy to be spoken to. His inheritance had brought with it the circle of fools who quiver with delight whenever the opportunity arises to be courted by someone's money. Thus Ramose' sole attraction became the source of all contempt given and received.

Unfortunately, Brosnan's position, cleverly calculated for isolation from the main thoroughfare of people, made evasion impossible. On the other side of the ballroom, amidst the small audience engaged by her natural charm, Evelyn observed with curious amusement, the inevitable encounter. She also saw that closely following Ramose was a gentleman she had never before seen, an elderly fellow who walked tall and decisively.

Brosnan looked at the man drawing alongside Ramose with faint recognition. Ramose lifted his eyebrows, and gestured as a slight noise leaked from his throat, an annoying sound invoking attention, signalling the inevitable diatribe was about to commence. Before that noise could be framed into words, Brosnan pre-empted the onslaught with a well-aimed enquiry toward Ramose' companion, "Excuse me sir. Your face stirs a memory. By any chance, do I know you?"

"Well, I hope you do! This is Justice Thorogood, *Sir* Justice Thorogood." Ramose injected, the sneer firing like a water pistol. Brosnan had happened upon his book, AfterMath; a challenging read about the proportions of existence, the subterranean influence of maths upon society and the probability of the existence of God. The book concludes with the statement, *"The serious mathematician is always seeking to prove the existence of God. Any notion or motion contrariwise is a mistake."*

Brosnan spent most of his calculated life purposefully committed to the opposite presupposition: maths is all the god we need: precise, all encompassing, unmoving, never-ending, and conclusive. He thought it improper for maths to be applied to anything metaphysical, and considered probability the lowest form of mathematics, as sarcasm is the lowest from of humour, and assumption the lowest form of knowledge.

Thorogood's apparent association with Ramose made Brosnan cautious. Yet, as Sir Justice spoke, "You are right in thinking that you know me, as I also know you." His demeanour felt embracing, and, above all, honest and unpretentious. Brosnan felt his guard lowering.

"Now, there is little privacy here, and I came tonight intending to speak with you," Then Sir Justice firmly suggested, "So, if you do not mind, Ramose, may you attend to your other guests and leave us to discuss what I am confident would be utterly unprofitable and unnatural to a man like yourself."

With that, Justice took Brosnan by the arm; and before anything more could be said, Ramose was left stranded, straining to hear Sir Justice Thorogood continue his discussion, "Indeed, I have been looking forward to our encounter for what seems like an e..." conversation faded into the noise of the crowd.

Evelyn watched, intrigued by the exchange, and made her way across the room to her cousin. His weaselly eyes, glaring from that pinched and narrowed face, remained fixed firmly on Brosnan standing on the portico, listening intently to a very enthusiastic Sir Justice.

"Who is that, Ramose?"

His gaze fixed, Ramose responded, "Why dear cousin, that's Sir Justice Thorogood. He's an ambassador from, hmm, from somewhere; just where escapes me momentarily. He turned up the other day and invited himself to tonight's party. Naturally, I agreed! He's quite the celebrity in some circles, you know, and with his credentials he can get through any door. But why he wants to converse with your husband baffles the beeswax out of me."

Evelyn drew near as the exchange approached its end, surprised, upon closer scrutiny, to discover the elderly fellow's mass of wavy white hair belied his age; he was much younger than she first thought. His voice similarly a harmonious mixture of the sage and the child: calm, firm, astute, penetrating, yet percolating and vibrant, "To find what you are searching for takes more than your wits." Justice elucidated, "True knowledge comes to you; though you search for it, you cannot find it. The best we can do is simply recognise it when and where it manifests. It materialises upon the willing mind; like magic, so to speak. So, it occurs among children, and poets, and all recognised genii. Through a simple application of attention, they see what evades the consciousness of the masses who are content to be told that what they see is all there is."

"I have little time for metaphysics, Holy Grails, or waiting for truth to come to me," Brosnan smiled congenially as Evelyn took his arm, "but I thank you for putting some unexpected interest into an otherwise dreary evening."

Politely they parted.

That was four months prior. Brosnan was never the same after that. And Evelyn blames Sir Justice for her husband's present disposition.

CHAPTER

Evelyn's Reprisal

When Brosnan finally slid under the sheets on that chill winter's night, Evelyn instinctively drew close. His cool body snatched her from slumber. Hazy eyes peered at the clock on the bedside table, and irritation sizzled, "It's 4:00am! Have you been working all this time?"

Faint insecurity, a flash of annoyance, a measure of confusion over the inexplicable merged and quivered in Brosnan's chest. No answer seemed reasonable; so, he put his arm around her, kissed her shoulder, and drifted into sleep.

Awake with the dawn, a crisp clear winter's morn, Brosnan could hear Evelyn busying herself in the background. By the time he finished dressing, the kitchen table was set with breakfast waiting. He applied himself to the task: toast, too much butter, poached eggs, bacon, and lots of coffee. The table delights, and the brilliant morning lustre sanctioned Brosnan's buoyant mood. How he had risen in such good humour after merely two hours sleep was an amusing question. He even caught his lips emitting an occasional whistle.

Evelyn's demeanour, however, did not display the songbird; she hadn't slept since Brosnan entered the bed, and her tension began probing for answers before he had finished his eggs. He attempted evasion, and failed; Evelyn would not let him off the hook until her interrogation finally pierced his skin.

Self-examination doesn't come easy for a man, and Brosnan could never be accused of adhering to the axiom "Know Thyself," but unexpectedly, under the piercing light of Evelyn's scrutiny, he acknowledged an inner tearing, some aspect of his personality was being stripped and searched. Hesitancy over exposing last night's episode was replaced by a longing to unburden his silent desperation revolving around the unnerving mystery of those catatonic seizures. Honesty awoke and won the battle. Having danced around the subject for ten minutes or so, Brosnan confessed, "My intention was to be in bed by 10:30, but something happened. Something I can't explain. I didn't make it out of the study until the time you woke."

Brosnan's customary self-assuredness had all the edge of a deflated basketball, and Evelyn, with her pensive eyes, understood immediately, "So, you had another spell! Blanked out again!"

"What do you mean?"

"You actually believe something can be happening to you without my knowing. I know you better than you know yourself."

"I, I don't know what you mean." His voice surrendered more defence than intended. If the truth be known, he wished to hear nothing at all of her meaning.

"Well, that evening, six months ago, when I found you on the floor of your study, your woven lie about falling from the third shelf of the library was unconvincing. You didn't fall at all, you blacked out. *I know!* Then there was the time I discovered you slumped over your books. Trying to rouse you was impossible. Until, just when the ambulance arrived, you surfaced, as though you'd never been asleep."

Brosnan sat, his eyes a little wider than usual. He could feel his ears blush as he realised his clever little ruse was proving him the fool fooling himself.

"I want to know what's going on Brosnan. What's wrong with you? What's wrong with us?"

Sitting at the kitchen table that crisp winters morn, the whole story unfolded, "Three years ago, was the first time it happened: I was in the library at Saint Simone, researching for an upcoming lecture. I was reading about the ancient Pythagoreans. Suddenly, a red light flashed across my eyes. With that, I lost two and a half hours. It just disappeared. Not as time does when you get engrossed in something interesting; No! No! No! It wasn't like that at all; a hundred and fifty minutes simply vanished. The arm supporting my head was numb, and there was drool on my beard. I checked my watch and realised I had been on the same page for over two hours; hadn't read more than three sentences." He continued providing a brief overview of several events, interspersed with occasional nervous laughter and positive speculation, "Last night's incident was the seventh occasion that I can recall, there may have been more."

Secrets told often bring relief with the sharing; Brosnan felt no such solace. It was right for him to be honest with Evelyn, and that he knew, but vulnerability had found its evolution in the sharing; submerged fears elevated, threatening to propel his pounding heart right out of his chest. Perhaps it was his recent sense of estrangement that brought about the disease? He loved his wife no less than in days past, but he was acutely aware of their differences, simultaneously admired and resented. At this moment, as in every moment he felt demand pull him away from the sanctuary of his solitary pursuits, resentment was their poison.

"Well, that does it!" Evelyn's voice, packaging a firm and resolute will, brought Brosnan out of himself. "You can't continue having these blackouts, figuring everything's all right. *It's not all right!* Look at you, you're forty years old going on sixty."

She wasn't mistaken. Not many years prior, Brosnan competed in the county's ultra-marathon and was a top twenty finisher. Now, he had neither time, fitness, nor desire for a lazy jog through the forest.

"Something's wrong." Evelyn counselled, "I'm phoning Blaise, and we're going to get to the bottom of this."

Resistance was useless. "Okay! but I don't need a doctor! In fact, outside of these confounded glitches, I have never felt better." He lied. As begrudging as Brosnan had determined to sound, Evelyn's ultimatum provided a modicum of relief. Rising from the table, he held her close; the familiar fragrance of her hair comforted him. Inarticulate feelings traversed the distance between their hearts, and Evelyn, though still bristling from their exchange, and somewhat bewildered by Brosnan's account, felt warmed by the connection that had long been absent.

CHAPTER 5

Saint Simone's Revolution

What Brosnan failed to admit, had failed himself to fully assimilate, were the subtle yet undeniable changes affecting the world around him. As the catatonic interruptions persisted, each emergence left him suspecting his environment was strangely altered. Last night's fall was no exception. Driving to the university, the sensation of change was definite, and Brosnan crept toward it as a child creeps toward the edge of a cliff.

St. Simone University was located a short distance from home, nestled in a broad valley on the outskirts of a quaint village bearing the same name; a town of historic significance dating back to the first millennium. The University was young in comparison to some establishments in the area, merely several centuries old: decisively Gothic, its incredible weight plunging deep into the earth upholding levitation that reached for the heavens; it was sublime, majestic, mystical. Above the tree line it towered, laced with ivy, imposing, resisting time and dominating space. Portions of the building's foundations had a pre-history, being the base of a monastery where The Valoria, The Order of Grey Hoods, a select group of peculiarly gifted monks were educated, trained, and commissioned to collect and protect various artefacts and sacred regions of early Christendom.

Brosnan turned into Sunnyvale Drive, enjoying the reassuring familiarity of rubber jouncing on cobblestone. Frosty fields shimmering in the morning sun danced past left and right, blending beyond into the deep green of Ravenswood Forest. Before him, through wisps of morning mist, loomed with characteristic solidity and permanence, St. Simone University. To him on that morning, the very stones of that façade, thronged with shouting faces and open mouths, cried out. In that enchanted moment a sense of thrill and awe erupted and surprised him. Not being poetically inclined, Brosnan was unaccustomed to such aesthetic pleasure. Evelyn alone had been able to stir his heart with anything that was remotely unscientific. Momentarily he cast his mind to questioning the uncommon response, leaving the safe ground that languished in responsible functionality and determinism, and allowed hidden memories of innocence and purity to surface. He was delighting in the blaze and blur of life, when phenomenally, connecting the dots, to his surprise it dawned that such apprehension had been his before. He recalled as a child he would walk through those very woods and feel the force of enchantment. Back then, Ravenswood was a magical forest; its enchantment remained. He nearly fell off the cliff.

Brosnan virtually leaped out of the Jag, then forced his mind toward the task ahead: two full sessions of advanced maths. The vision had lifted, but the mood remained.

Eight students were in attendance. The semester commenced with a group much larger, twenty-two in all, but attrition had taken its toll; Brosnan's regimen was not for the faint hearted. Nevertheless, the gifted and arduous thrived under his tutelage; there really was no alternative. In a university famous for its pedagogy in mathematical application, Brosnan was the best in his field, and taught what could be offered nowhere else in the country.

They watched for twenty minutes or so as Brosnan chalked extensively on the board. It was an inconclusive equation, one he'd been working on for many years, and there were no expectations, on his part, of any student deciphering it. With no logical reason for presenting the insolvable to the class, it was definitely not part of his usual curriculum, his assumed reasoning lay in the process; it would be a beneficial exercise for all; and those who were particularly gifted could perhaps provide a fresh approach to the problem.

Brosnan addressed the group with customary sobriety, "What's wrong with this? You have four hours to come up with the answer: Make it elegant! Make it simple!" With half a smile, he quipped, "Good luck!"

Amidst a flurry of paper, muffled laughter and the odd groan, they settled to the task. Brosnan also gave the equation the sum of his attention. Gradually, the unexpected happened: All morning, a subsonic hum, a subliminal tone had been bearing him up. Slowly, ever so slowly, as the class was entering its third hour, that tone reverberated throughout his whole being, and then the dawning came. He acknowledged that in the car a realisation of an alternate manner of observation arrived: Here, Brosnan *understood!* Observation had moved from comprehension to apprehension; he was seeing things with lucidity, all things. Now, without demanding, or displacing any mathematical rigor, he was addressing the equation, and looking into it with uncomplicated clarity. It struck him that for the first time in his adult life he had the answer without the exertion of rational energy.

Initially, he concealed his surging thrill, only the most perceptive would have observed. His "scientific" approach to life could never anticipate this. He was becoming aware of an interior awakening that made sense of life, as if a severed nerve within had reforged its connection. Again, he looked at the board, seven years of sweat and blood evaporated, leaving the answer clear and precise. Brosnan could no longer contain his exhilaration, "Eureka!" Before the students could close their bewildered mouths, he exited the room.

CHAPTER

Surprise! Surprise! Surprise!

Brosnan returned home early that day, surprising Evelyn, who, after a few moments inquired, "Well what did Blaise have to say?"

Brosnan hedged. Whilst expecting immediate scrutiny he was nevertheless bothered by its arrival. Evelyn pursued him down the hallway and into the kitchen. He picked at the food on the table, aware of Evelyn's eyes burrowing deeper into his conscience. Knowing there would be no reprieve until he surrendered, Brosnan breathed deeply and confessed, "I, err, I didn't go."

He braced for impact; instead, there was silence. Faltering, Brosnan glanced sheepishly and saw a tear burst the bank of Evelyn's eye. He stumbled for words, for a reason, but none would come. In their place he filled his mouth with a bread stick.

"With yet another piece of diabolical calculus you have reduced me to the lowest common denominator!" Evelyn cried. (Brosnan quickly discarded the impulse to correct Evelyn's mixed mathematical metaphors.) "Can't you tell I'm scared? Can't you see me? What I'm going through? Something's wrong! You're withdrawn, untouchable; I can't seem to break through to you anymore. Add to that these awful blackouts. I want to know what's going on, and you barely talk to me."

"It's not that I don't want to talk; I just don't know what to say. I was going to see Blaise, I really was; but he blew right out of my mind somehow. Anyway, I don't need help; at least not his kind of help. Instead, this afternoon I phoned Justice Thorogood. He wants to see me; he wants to see us."

Evelyn's emotion changed up a gear, "Who? What possible help could the nutty professor provide? You met him four months ago, and, as far as I can tell, you've been worse for the meeting, further off in your own world than ever before."

"He's a good man, Evelyn; you said so yourself after you saw him at that party. And you know your intuition is rarely wrong."

The tension was tearing at Evelyn's face. Brosnan frantically attempted to talk the strain away, "I phoned him because of something he said to me at Ramose' dinner party: He said, 'Truth has little to do with intelligence. You do not work it out; it simply comes to you.' Well, today it happened, just like he said. As I was driving the car to work, I realised everything appeared utterly different. Then that formula I have been working on for years and years, it just came together, out of the blue. And when I was talking to the students today, it wasn't just about facts and figures; I really engaged. It was incredible." Brosnan's words were struggling to keep pace with his mind, "Then Thorogood asked me if I had been experiencing any strange events, anything like time warps or waking up in strange places, or unexplainable visions. I asked him, 'What do you mean?' He simply answered, 'I know!' and, 'We must get together as soon as possible.' So, he is coming over for supper tonight."

Evelyn stared, unimpressed and overwhelmed; her gaping mouth, the hollow into which her damp cheeks flowed. She wasn't sharing Brosnan's enthusiasm but accepted the situation with a look of abject resignation verging on shock, and some pensive inquiry as to the tone of the evening and the nature of the visit.

As the seething moment subsided, Brosnan looked at the kitchen clock, "Come on, we've got time. I'll help get something together."

Evelyn looked at herself and despaired at being ill prepared for guests, let alone an ambassador.

"Why, you look absolutely ravishing; picture perfect!" Brosnan took her by the waist. Evelyn would have enjoyed this uncommon frolic around the kitchen, had she not been simultaneously dumbfounded and infuriated. Before she could open her mouth, Brosnan sealed his little conquest, "After we've finished here, I'll set the table and you can freshen up for our guest."

CHAPTER 7

The Ancient Prophecy

The doorbell rang at half past seven. Expectation played no part in moderating the surprise Brosnan displayed at the sound, for it seemed to him unusually loud for such a small bell. Evelyn looked at her husband quizzically; he was not generally so over reactive.

Brosnan took Sir Justice' scarf, coat, and hat, dusting off white flakes of snow, and escorted him through the lounge. Evelyn's reservations came with a cordial offering, some of her homemade mead warm from the hearth. The fire and elixir did their work, stealing the winter chill from Sir Justice without and within, and loosening his mouth so to speak, "That's a mighty fine brew you have concocted, Lady Evelyn. I doubt I have tasted finer." Evelyn, flushed at the formality associated with her name, invited him through to the dining room where dinner was prepared.

Affable and gentle in conversation, Justice Thorogood was clearly enjoying himself, complimenting every morsel of the modest meal. Eventually, his winsome manner unravelled Evelyn's cautious disposition and she relaxed.

Brosnan, also was uncommonly attentive. Quite some time had lapsed since he had taken such delight in Evelyn's demeanour, her relaxed elegance, her occasional whimsy, her romanticism. They dined in this favoured state for hours, until Justice broached the subject, "Come now, we really must talk about your pursuits; and of course, those blackouts. So much to discuss. I do believe that after tonight you will both feel much the better about things."

Brosnan proceeded to reiterate the series of events as explained that morning to Evelyn, adding, "Nothing of what transpires during the unconscious state remains with me, but, the very night of our meeting at that party, I had a dream, and when I awoke, I remembered everything. A wave was coming toward me, not of water, but fire. Along with it I heard, no, felt more than heard, the sound of metal striking metal, like a blacksmith beating down on his anvil. I would not think it important, except that I've had the same dream on numerous occasions, once while exiting one of those subliminal states. Normally I remember nothing at all when I return from them, but for some reason that catatonic condition made the dream particularly vivid."

With this new edition to the story, Evelyn's lips opened slightly, losing the colour that rushed to the lobes of her ears. "I'm sorry I didn't tell you, darling," Brosnan appealed, "but the dream makes me feel as though I'm drowning, and I wished to avoid any pillow-talk cross-examination." Her lips said nothing; her eyes said plenty.

Justice broke into the tension, "It is late, and I have overstayed my welcome; but let me reassure you, Lady Evelyn, and you also, Brosnan, though you seem less perturbed by these events than your dear wife, I can offer some explanation for the arrested states occasioning your life these past few years, and provide you with insight into what has been taking place while you are captured therein. For now, rest assured, little is wrong with your anomalous transactions, in fact, everything is right with them."

With that, Sir Justice' eyes brightened and he laughed such a hearty laugh that it infected Brosnan and Evelyn, momentarily dispelling the heaviness that Brosnan's self-exposure had syphoned into their evening. "One more thing before I take my leave." Into his bag, Justice rummaged, extracting a tube from which he withdrew an aged and worn document. At that moment the clock struck eleven, and, as happened with the ringing of the doorbell, Brosnan startled, this time throwing his hands over his ears, "That clock is so loud," he grimaced, "it clangs like the old church bell, and we are all inside it."

Paying Brosnan's dramatics no heed, Justice carefully unrolled the ancient scroll. It was inscribed with language neither Brosnan nor Evelyn had seen before, in appearance, somewhere between Hebrew and Arabic. Sir Justice gazed at their faces with childlike delight, "Allow me to translate it for you:"

Lo it is written of me in the scroll of the book…
Before the Heavens and Earth were formed…
In incipient innocence was I born
Pure and undefiled, enlightened liberty
The Song of Life weaving Solidarity

But one more luminous, displaced and torn
Who in pride despised all natural form
In presumption's madness he arose
To claim the crown and take the Throne…
Who reaching for the Sceptre fell
Into the darkened citadel…

And to my everlasting shame,
I was deceived, and falling fell
With him Into dark and impure flame
Torment's abyssynic cell

And I who was,
was not.

In that chamber of darkness long
Eternal is my falling
Worse am I, deaf to the Song
Wherefore my heart is Longing
Disfigured ears attuned to strains
Of nature's enigmatic chains
My soul burning, insatiable desire
Worms do feast upon my fire
Dawnless night, a marish dream
Miserable emptiness… The silent scream
But there is yet hope,
Though it seems for a fool,
And it is not the hope of me
For the Ancient Song is filled
With unrequited Prophecy

"Yea! A Voice is heard in the darkened haunting
In the caverns of the damned Light brighter than
The seven suns doth shine
The Chamber Illuminated, no longer deforming
All is reforming in the fulness of time"

So, there is hope
Though I see it not
For I who once was
Am not!

Thorogood was bursting with anticipation, as though he were a child expecting a second round of dessert. Brosnan, with unexpected discomfort, became defensive, "Begging your pardon, Sir Justice, but producing this roll of old paper has not helped explain my situation one fraction. In fact, I am now wondering precisely why you are here at all."

"Be at peace young friend. Though you see no correlation now, all will be made plain in the telling. Distress began nibbling at your innards as I commenced reading from the parchment, did it not?"

Brosnan's eyes signalled it was so.

Justice enthused, "That is because this prophecy is about *you*."

Brosnan was unprepared for the intense scrutiny of the moment; he felt a searchlight was hunting him down. Thorogood adjusted his glasses, he was about to continue reading, but Brosnan held his hand, "I really think I've heard enough."

"Don't worry," Sir Justice consoled, "the story is about to get better."

However, a second factor was bearing down upon Brosnan, demanding immediate attention: Throughout the reading, Brosnan could hear noise, initially some distance away, but always drawing closer; it sounded like a crowd of people storming up the street of their peaceful village. When he commented concerning the disturbance, Evelyn, whose mind and heart were probing the poem's purpose, secretly suspected her husband's magnificent mind had finally flipped, whilst Sir Justice' face, accustomed as he was to serendipity, waxed mischievous. By the time Brosnan stood to investigate, that approaching noise clattered and rumbled and roared, until he was sure the mob had rammed through the door and was now inside his house. That was when a flashing wave of red light, thick as blood, flooded the room, and suddenly he looked upon a thoroughly alternate world.

CHAPTER

The Man With No Name

He's mad! Worse, he's a savage! Nothing good will come of this. "You can't do anything with a mad savage."

"Quiet, Suso! Do you think I, and the might of Moranor, went to hell and back for nothing? This *mad savage* is not what he appears, and you would do well to mind your tongue before you multiply stupidity."

Suso berated himself for his hasty lips and spoke more soberly, "Begging your pardon, Uriel: Why have we paid such a great price for this?" Suso accentuated his doubtful inquiry with a shrug that tossed my pathetic body one way and then the other.

"Never you mind, Suso. Question me no further. All will be revealed at the appropriate time. Now, take him to the tower, and place him in the light. And be careful to lock the door. I charge you to be his safeguard. If any harm comes to him…"

Suso butted in with a pledge, "I will care for him as for my own life."

"He is not yet safe from himself. Until he is, the whole world dwells on the verge of destruction." With that Uriel went his way, and I went the other, Suso hauling me higher, and higher, muttering under his breath something about

Uriel's beard. Throughout that conversation my eyes saw nothing except the colour red, deep as blood.

Sometime later I heard Uriel's voice calling me, "Orson! I order you to leave your dark tomb and come into Light. I command scales of darkness to fall from your eyes. I lay claim upon your mind and return it to sanity."

I shuddered and lurched; powerful words were wrenching me up and into my skin. I left crimson darkness behind and opening my eyes, saw a face before me, frighteningly strong, yet impeccably kind, with pensive and sympathetic eyes searching through silvery hair. His was the first human face I'd seen since losing my mind.

"Do I know you?" Speaking required terrific effort.

"You do not even know yourself, how can you know me, or anyone else? I am Uriel: The Light! The Voice! I have brought you out of darkness. For too long you have slept; now I call you to action. The battle for your life is at hand. I urge you to fight for soundness of mind and the liberation of your soul."

"How can I? I have been weak far too long. What you ask is beyond me. How can I fight for sanity, when voices haunt me? They drive me mad! And do not mock me with tempting taunts of liberty; freedom is vain hope goading a tortured soul."

"Do not think liberty a torture," Uriel admonished, "for freedom is already yours, though you see it not. Granted, it seems impossible to have vision when imprisoned by darkness year upon year; but to this end I have been sent, that you might hear and see again, and thereby find the life you lost."

"You seek to lift me on a wave of hope only to dash me against rocks of perdition. I cannot! I have tried and tired, and become the devil's plaything."

Ignoring my vain assumptions, Uriel gave me this charge: "You must find out who you are. This is your foremost duty. Everything depends upon finding that which is lost."

"Why can't you tell me and be done with it?"

"Were I to tell you, you would not receive it, you would not believe it, you cannot even hear it. Such knowledge is too great to bear, for with a name comes accountability and obligation. You must find it for yourself. It may comfort you to hear that I know who you are. For now, put your trust in that."

I pleaded with him, "Help me!"

"I am here to guide and support, but you are the one who has forgotten your self; you lost your name and you alone can find it. Know also, if you had not answered to another name, you would never have lost your own."

Opaque red liquid spilled over conscious attention and my mind almost left me; I strained to make a sole request, "Can you take me to a different room? The light, it drives me mad."

I held on for the answer, my face a distortion, my breath failing, my body a cold, clammy, shivering, weak and pathetic appendage of a lost and forgotten world.

"It is your demons, not the light, that induces the maniacal drive. Without the light you will never heal. Now face your task and chance your hand."

Suso was left to suffer my raving and raging with a parting command, "Give his eyes three hours of sunlight every day. Then wrap them in muslin."

Uriel's voice held me, but with his parting, darkness came like a deluge. A pallid hand wrapped around my ankle and I fell. More hands reached for me. Possessing no strength to resist, I surrendered. They pulled me under, through the floor, and into the deep darkness below, where I returned to the tormented sleep of eternal oblivion.

In the inner crucible, pain became my friend; for with every searing press of flame and every piercing of my flesh, suffering reminded me I was still alive. My friend brought me to my senses. I was being hoisted into the air, my back to the ceiling; small hooks threading my skin were connected to wires and by them I hung suspended like a marionette. Orchestrating all this was The Ugly. He preferred to be addressed as Dorran-ap-Lusdburn, the Prince of Darkness;

but I called him what he was, Chemosh, the hideous one. Chemosh was he who gave life to death. Lord, he was, over the living dead. He paraded the halls of his callous kingdom where bodies dangled like decorations from ceiling and walls, whilst others lay strewn over the dungeon floor. His two pets were permanently chained to their post; dogs, large as bears, with glistening black coats; feasting as opportunity provided on the flesh of anything within reach.

Chemosh considered me his finest work for I had lived through the life and death of hundreds of others. I was his trophy. He saw my eyes open and his hollow laughter filled the tomb with rotting wind, and my mind with emptiness. The Ugly prided himself in the art of pain; his skill lay in balancing a victim over the reaper's scythe, holding on to life and praying for death. When he thought I had grown accustomed to the hooks, he placed a fire under my belly, lowering me upon it until the blisters bulged. I would then be taken to another evil invention, and another; a continually evolving product of dark cunning.

Darkened flame was the light of that realm, producing neither warmth nor illumination. It made everything take on a scarlet hue. High, and barred, a solitary window plastered with mud never acknowledged the light of day. As I saw no light, there was no time or change of season; nothing but an eternal, twisted cycle of torture, a shifting, heartless nightmare wherein I passed along a production line of agony. For my lot, I was born in suffering and I was doomed to endure it forever.

I know not how long I remained in that Cimmerian citadel before there came a shift in the order of things, before the unexpected took place and the timeless deep was somehow pierced. When it came, I took hold of it with all my miserable being.

CHAPTER

What Light From Yonder Window Breaks?

F ever diluted the energy of my morbid frame until I became a sweaty slab of meat on the carving table. I welcomed the vacant rest of insentience.

Chemosh was watching; always watching. An involuntary twitch surfaced whenever I lost sensibility; it amused him. His laughter verged on hunger. He did not feed often, but once he chose, he invariably swallowed more than he could chew; and the display proved him to be more beastly than his beasts. The Ugly sidled to a table several paces away which benched another slab of meat, the carcass of a huge pig, and set to, consuming more than half of the animal along with several buckets of ale which induced the customary lazy slumber that on this occasion he would lament.

My mind was drifting in and out of lucidity. A wrenching pain tugged on my gut where bowels, having been extricated from a jagged hole in my abdomen, draped and dangled limply over the edge of the table. It was that pain, the kind that pulls on a soul's entire existence, which triggered my waking; and that same pain thrust me back into oblivion; the terrible demagogue pulling and pushing me in and out of the ocean's deep; sleeping and waking, drowning and hanging; and then floating. As my pupil floated down to the corner of my eye, I could see a tongue flickering, trying to catch a lick of my entrails. The dogs preferred live meat if they could get it. His nose came within a hair's-breadth of my hanging gut before his eyes rolled in the direction of the collar as the chain choked the hound's huge neck.

There, in the hopelessness of that hellish stronghold, a phenomenon occurred: As I lay motionless, immobilised and traumatised, extraordinary warmth flashed upon my face. It flashed and disappeared, and then returned in even greater glory. This was not the stinging heat of dark flame. I had long grown accustomed to that; the boils, the pussy blisters, the disfiguring and scarring of my outer shell. No, this warmth was healthy, nourishing, and therefore doubly shocking. I was afraid to move, afraid the good would stop, scared to open my eyes lest the radiance turn out to be a figment of imagination. Or, perhaps, here was a new instrument of evil, creating pleasure so exquisite the anguish of withdrawal would be all the more severe.

I have no notion how long I lay there where a moment lasts an eternity. The warmth did not retract and its goodness was slowly but surely seeping through to my bones. Motionless, I absorbed every blissful particle. Stars danced before me as the luminary substance penetrated my tight lid eyes. I dare not look, yet I could wait no longer. I held my breath and risked a peek. High above, higher than could possibly be determined, a dazzling brightness penetrated a fissure in the ceiling; light was streaking through the darkened cell, pure, concentrated goodness, that purposefully sought me out and found me. The depth of my need was perfectly matched by the height of that grace. Oh, the bliss of being awakened to something good, to again feel the gentle caress of pure virtue. I basked in delight; I exhilarated in it!

Suddenly, paranoia wrapped its callous hand around my throat: Surely, he will wake, and seeing, extinguish the light, before venting vengeance upon me.

However, he did not wake; The Ugly remained sprawled across his table, with darkness shrouding him still. His beasts also, having gorged on their keeper's leftovers, lay sleeping, fitfully satisfied under the master's table.

Meanwhile, the crack became a small window and I could see a raven taking to thick clay with beak, claw, and severe determination, piercing a hole where no hole should be. Radiant light grew brighter, and with it my resolve. Emotion coursed through me; a powerful mixture of gratitude and hope combined to give me strength. For the first time in that dark abyss I was able to steer my mind away from suffering. Potency infiltrated my soul. I had not felt strong for an eternity. Rage? Yes! Rage, and anger and feeble bitterness, but never strength.

It was then I discovered that my feet and hands were lacking their adamantine chains. Chemosh had been lax. And who could blame him, there had been no disturbance of his domain in recent history, not since The Pantokrator had entered and cracked the prison's foundations. That crack descended deeper than hell, deeper than even Chemosh would dare go.

So, it was that circumstance and opportunity kissed each other. The unthinkable had arrived, the demand of choice was upon me; I could fly, and I would soar. Gritting my teeth, I gathered my intestines and pushed them back inside my abdomen, "Phssst!" That sudden unintentional influx of air sucking pain through clenched teeth broke the golden silence. The dogs stirred, and seeing me standing, lurched with frightening ferocity. Though knowing the chain would cut short their reach, I nevertheless stumbled backward. The Ugly lifted his head and beheld my face glowing under the sun. His features distorted into a comic mosaic of madness and blubbering confusion, and just as rapidly returned to their former sinister repulsiveness. His frenzied scream echoed through the chamber.

CHAPTER 10

The Shadow-Beast

Unexpectedly, uncommon courage filled my soul; and with it, the fog of conflicting emotions heretofore enveloping me evaporated, and I could see clearly. Four floors I descried skirting the sides of the cavern; here and there a flight of stairs, here and there a ladder. Beyond my sight and at the extremity of my heart's vision, I saw the doorway to freedom. My moment had come, and I made myself move.

"Get him!" Chemosh screeched in an agony of terror.

His dogs reached the end of their tether, but they were not the ones he was inciting. The dungeon's floor began moving, heaving, as though breathing. Lifeless bodies stirred and took on a ghoulish hue reminiscent of the hands that pulled me under the tomb. Leaving the sun's radiant beam behind, I reached a huge block of stone, which was the foot of the ascending staircase. I mounted it just as the first hellraker rose to his feet and set to the hunt.

Climbing those naked and numberless steps was sweetly arduous; each lifting leg pulled at my innards, shunting intense pain throughout my body, yet each surge was scintillatingly optimistic, full of anticipation, replete with the thrill of escape. Using one hand to dam my spilling gut and the other to steady the climb, I spurred myself upward, leaving behind the raucous, clambering ghouls and the bellowing blasts of The Ugly; until eventually I stood triumphant upon the first landing.

My eyes spanned the terrain, but capturing even a faint outline of the next flight of stairs proved beyond all sight; it became obvious that in this place, space, as well as time, was grossly distorted. I turned my attention to the immediate and surveyed the arena before me. It was a battlefield: scattered pieces of armour and weaponry; swords and bucklers and shields, crossbows and lances and axes, helmets and breastplates and war hammers, the barren bones of fallen horses and their fallen riders. This is where battles are fought and lost. A yellow mist wafted over the ground. It swirled occasionally, disturbed by an invisible presence. Fear is the root of all war, and fear filled this place.

Agitation scurried behind. A glance down the staircase counted several ghouls narrowing the gap. The sight of them spurred me onto the obstacle course, toward where I hoped I would locate the ascent to higher, and presumably safer, ground. It was not easily negotiated. In addition to the scattered wreckage there were many pits and cracks hidden under the yellow mist, and the heavy fear of that place displaced all available light.

Haste betrayed me. I fell sprawling upon the floor. Sulphurous vapour rushed into my lungs. My throat constricted, my stomach spilled, and my head sought the refuge of unconsciousness. I was reeling, but fought off the stupor and gathered myself for another assault upon the battlefield.

At that moment, into my determination there intruded a sound, a deep throaty rasp that felt perfectly compatible with the murky, menacing mood. The only thing on that theatre of war incompatible with its dread disposition was me. I was above it and beyond it, as a brave man is above and beyond the dragon, or a noble man is above and beyond the world. I was not simply alive, I had something more than mere existence - I was a man! I searched for the origin of that fitful gurgle, but for some time could not tell from whence it came.

Then, in a swirl of vomitus yellow, the mist before me began to shape itself into the form of personality, a shadow from the depths of shadow. Not twenty paces ahead, a human form, twice as tall as I but half my width, looked to approach me. Instinctively I withdrew; whereupon the human-shadow emitted a moan that filled the air with sadness, and my mind with annihilation. As that sound collapsed into hell, so the tall thin shadow descended ground-ward like melting wax, and there upon the floor, through a series of contortions it took on the guise of a beast. The guardian of this realm had come to penetrate my heart, to petrify my every movement, and seal me from escape.

With stealth, the shadow-beast circled, slowly surrounding me with its dread, entwining vapour round my throat, constricting the air, freezing my mind, paralysing my body. Moments prior, I was invincible; now, terror threatened to overwhelm every part of me. I feared a shadow in the house of wax.

Mesmerised, petrified, it was the ghouls who saved me. They reached the top of the stairs with too much commotion, and their noise broke the tapestry of terror the shadow-beast was weaving. Quickly I scrambled, rummaging over the ground for a weapon to defend myself. I found a mace, but I doubted my strength to wield it; then my hand felt the blade of a sword. Perfect! I made a demand upon my legs and charged at the shadow. It reared, then leaped into darkness.

The suffocating fear abated without entirely subsiding. A none-too-distant howl, the evil portent of the shadow-beast's contriving, informed me I would meet him again. In the background, I could see the ghoulish hellrakers surging towards me; but in the chamber slowly brightening they became more ghostly, less real, and consequently less threatening. Still, with no intention of being overrun by them, my getaway resumed.

I know not how far I journeyed, but I ran as best I could, until finally my heart soared when the next flight of stairs appeared upon the frontier. Though I outpaced the ghouls, the howling seemed closer, louder, until I thought the noise of that rapacious beast would bring the walls of the chamber crashing down. Abruptly, I was confronted by shocking silence, a vacuum, as loud as the howl it replaced. I should have paid it more heed; but I saw my goal and willed my body onward against the noiseless void.

I was mid-stride when my feet went from under me. It was the shadow; its tail whipped behind my knees and I toppled like felled lumber into a toxic abyss. The mist invading my nose and mouth instantly made my lungs and throat feel like they were slashed by a thousand razors. My eyes swelled till I could barely see. Fallen, fatigued, shivering; yet persevering. Against cold exhaustion, I twisted through the swirling vapour, scrambling frantically until eventually I stood, and, displaying my sword, challenged that frozen eternal shade which confounded my escape. Trembling words sliced through my throat like a glacier and shattered upon the ground.

The shadow rushed toward me and I dodged. It came again and caught me just above the ankle, claws gouging deeper than my flesh. I ripped my leg away and blood flowed. Though I slashed, and thrashed, and hacked with the sword, there was no substance to the shadow upon which I might affect damage.

The beast leaped and fell on me: All claws and teeth, tearing and biting and ripping. I was tossed and torn and defenceless; each gouge and laceration infused itself to me, filling me with icy barrenness. As I absorbed its emptiness, from me the beast leeched substance, and with substance weight; so much weight it threatened to crush me. I thought the worst; until the first ghoul arrived.

The hellrakers seemed totally unaware that they were being shadowed by several more shadow-beasts; one, in fact, for every ghoul. The beasts emerged from darkness and set about stalking them; the hunters became the hunted. Little by little, as they were closing on their prey, the beasts became aware of each other; and, with little fondness shared, agitation flared. My shadow turned and wailed his threat to the others. When they failed to heed his warning, he gave them his total attention. I was flung aside; the tearing claws made a popping sound as they were sucked out of my skin. The beasts were returning threat for threat until they could no longer resist the fight. There, between the ghouls and me, the shadows savaged each other.

I took the opportunity to crawl away, keeping one eye on the mêlée. Thanks to the life sucked from me, my beast was larger and stronger than the other beasts, which were vacant shadows in comparison; quickly they were torn and quickly devoured. The ghouls, halted temporarily by the brouhaha, soon discovered they were next in line. As the beast turned on them, they railed their torment; not in concern for personal safety, for their flesh felt neither pleasure nor pain, but because they were unable to reach me. If they were to spend eternity in hell they wanted as much company as possible. They screamed with the tearing darkness. Some leaped over the ledge and fell into fire. What was left of the others remained scattered across the war-scape's floor.

The raven had done his job; light from that lone window was enlightening the chamber, unveiling the condition of hell. Peering over the ledge I saw pandemonium! a horrible chaotic struggle of the properties of nature, a swirling, churning, burning torment; the inversion of everything good and orderly and beautiful; Nihil! It was unbearable and I felt as though I were being inverted, turned inside out. Nonetheless, I could not tear my eyes from the madness. My head suddenly reeled and I swooned, falling mesmerised toward the yawning abyss into which I gazed too long. That was when another light, a different light, from an alternate source, caught my attention. It was a sword set in stone, tilting precariously from the edge of the ledge, vibrating, as though it had just been plunged into the rock, and it sang with its own sun dancing upon the blade. As I fell, with utmost desperation, I reached for that bright steel; or perhaps it reached for me. Somehow, I found myself dangling between heaven and hell, my fingers wrapped tight around the sword's hilt. That luminous blade offered me its strength; power flowed through my soul, warming all that the shadow-beast had chilled. With that strength I turned my eyes from hell's horror and clawed my way onto the ledge.

Back to the stairs I ran. I stumbled up a few, and then a few more. The beast, having dealt with the ghouls, quickly returned to finish me off. It either knew not, or cared not, that in my hand I possessed a sword of light, and launched itself into the air. Once again, I felt those claws in my leg. Together, we tumbled down the stairs, and, as we did, the blazing blade I held in my hand disappeared. I feared I had lost it, or the beast had destroyed it. Upon slamming into the ground, I discovered the sword was buried deep in the beast's chest. Light pierced the shadow's black heart and it wailed its last dread wail.

As I retrieved my sword, from its wound there streamed a flood of putrid blood, producing a glacial tide that flowed like treacle across the ground before surging over the ledge. Chemosh saw the black waterfall spilling into his basement, and, to the sound of his tormented screams, I recommenced my ascent.

CHAPTER 11

A Woman Clothed With The Sun

Abruptly, the cold stone ceased and in its place a ladder stretched. The rungs passed clumsily under my feet; a weary and protracted ascent. The last rung of the ladder saw the resumption of more granite; one flinty step after another, until fatigue stole me from my task and ushered me into exhausted slumber. There, in my dungeon, where erstwhile nightmares had been my portion, there walked a shimmering ecstasy - A woman came to me clothed in the sun; her flaxen hair cascaded like a waterfall, her deep blue eyes were as pensive pools pulling me in, her voice was music, her skin luminous, and her name was Charitas, daughter of the dawn, the giver of life and love. She took my breath away, and evermore I would love her. She fed me fruit from the Tree of Life, and over me she poured Living Water. Then sweet Charitas sang:

Al adure aron dularriman marandi thanu
Kainarr milath des-na kallar sannu-lambana

On the wings of her voice, I soared into the heavens, and though her language was not of this world, nevertheless, I understood:

PARALLEL WORLDS

True Love stronger than death
Her unceasing kiss
Melting the rock, the unresembling heart
Her sweet sigh the Breath of Life
Are yours together in the meeting
Of damnable and dangerous liaisons
Where doom you face and choosing choose
The singularly noble path that's true
To One you did before refuse
Ere now in solidarity remain
Ne're to wander from again
For the Living Flame doth purge you
Of manifold and disparate burnings
True heart thus changed becomes Her splendour
And through Love's kiss you are afire
Wholly simplified to one desire
And all your desire is for Me

Kneeling, Charitas placed her hand on my gaping wound, kissed my lips, and continued singing:

Gone are the days of sadness
The dawning has begun
Before the sun doth rise above
All evil is undone
And when all is unsaid and all is unsung
Surely wisdom and power and light
Go before you all the days of your life
Surely goodness and mercy shall follow
Redeeming the deeds of the night

I opened my eyes, my wounds were healed, my fever soothed, and I was strong.

CHAPTER 12

Nehushtan's Fury

Standing upon the second level, I surveyed the great cavern wall that arched toward the horizon where the next flight of stairs would be located. Still under the soothing enchantment of Charitas, it was with some shock that within ten paces I walked into a barrier of odorous death. The reason was soon apparent, for there before me, piled high against the escarpment, were carcasses, some animal, others human; dead things, that nevertheless possessed life; human and beast were joined as one, rising into a mound of putrid rottenness that stood higher than I; a repulsive living amalgam, throbbing, moving, breathing, heaving.

The landing was barely twenty feet wide, so I was compelled to negotiate the narrows and suffer a closer inspection of the creature. Slowly, I advanced. The smell was abusing the air. Drawing near the pulsing mass, I discovered the cause of its life apparent, for the carcasses were worked by worms, hundreds of them, large and pale as death, moiling their way through the meat, feasting and turning the monster over and over in their interminable hunt for flesh. The worms seemed blind and paid me no heed; interest rested solely in their gorging.

With nerves harnessed I manoeuvred past the worming knoll. My skin prickled with nervous apprehension: Something nefarious knew of my presence; I could sense eyes watching. Suddenly, the wall alongside the worms was rent from top to bottom. Wind blew upon my face, rapidly developing into a malicious gale; and there behind the wind a serpent with seven heads rushed toward me. It was a titan, a hydra: She was Nehushtan, harlot of the underworld, whose lust for mayhem and desolation was equalled solely by her thirst for power and flesh. I had climbed into her domain.

Nehushtan rose to power with the dawn of time and made herself queen under the mountain. She possessed subtlety and could weave herself into any form necessary to entrance her victim; but all fool's eyes, foolish enough to entertain her wiles, were undone. Never would she reveal her true likeness until her fangs were sunk deep into flesh and her prey was bloated with poison. Their carcass would then be dragged into her lair and cast upon the mound where the worms, her children, spawn of her lust, were fattened and nurtured for the end of time, when they would end all that is good.

Upon sight of me making bold my escape, Nehushtan arose in a rage, spitting her vehement hatred of life. However, that Jezebel was more dangerous when subtle, and I evaded her first violation. She raised herself tall and towering, her poisonous fangs were drooling. My back was pressed against the wall. I was sensing my strength, conviction steeling me for the attack; and I was wielding the sword of light. 'Pride,' I thought, 'would be her undoing.' I did not wait long, for with all her heads surrounding, she descended like an avalanche. I brandished the sword right to left, left to right, and three of her heads went tumbling. Nehushtan roared and reared; fountains of dark blood spewed from her snaking wounds. Wings were unfolded, wherewith she took flight, leaving the severed heads thrashing and snapping at my feet. Nehushtan alighted upon a precipice some thirty feet above and waited purposefully. There I beheld each truncated member give birth to not one but two heads; so now she had ten in all, joining together in an awful shrieking symphony. It was not her pride that undid Nehushtan, but my own that was the end of me. In vain I thought that I, by my own strength and cunning, could bring down the many heads of lust. Instead, I granted the beast increased powers of annihilation. Once all her remaking was finished, she looked at me and held me in contempt. My arrogance judged me. Desolation laughed at me. There is no slaying this beast; in vain would I spend my strength. My bane grows before my very eyes; returning she comes changed and bearing sisters with her.

Senseless, witless, clueless, I acknowledged one thing at that moment, my hatred of the hydra. I was determined not to become another trophy of her lust. Mustering all my conviction, I broke free from her trance and flailed my sword at the mound of Nehushtan's children, slicing through them again, and again, and again. Some escaped the blazing blade but plenty were cut asunder; and unlike their mother, they had not the severing's remedy.

Nehushtan was livid, and leaping from her perch, she shredded the air with a shriek. Then she came for me like a tempest. From her belly a web spat; it adhered to my arm and yanked me into the air. I was lifted high above the landing, a limp puppet on a string. Impulsively I cut through the sticky thread and plummeted to the floor. Rattled, yet not wrecked, I forced my body up and rushed into the crack from whence she first emerged.

Down, down, down I ran into the bowels of the earth, pursued by Nehushtan's lurid fury. Hours, maybe days passed, but I would not stop, and she would not relent. I ran until my lungs would burst, I ran until every muscle and fibre in my body threatened collapse, I ran into exhaustion and out the other side, I ran until the ground under my feet grew warm, and the fires burned around me. And there, in the bowels of the earth, the chase was brought to an abrupt termination. Ahead, a solid wall of hewn rock, fashioned by the ancients into an impenetrable barrier, faintly shimmered with a light of its own. I wheeled around to face the serpent closing fast. Never before had Nehushtan been so provoked, and she sought to spew her retched fury all over me. I held my ground, courage and fear contending for my heart. Sword in hand, its light aglow, I recognised its luminosity possessed a kinship with the rocks behind. In fact, the glow of that ancient stone was co-responding to the presence of the blade. Instinctively I took the sword and with its hilt struck the rock. The sound made was a wonder: strong as the earth, high as the mountains, full as the ocean, the perfect and comprehensive tone of the Tintinnabuli. Suddenly, in the eyes of the serpent there blinked a doubt; she hesitated, and I saw it. I struck the rock again, and again, until music filled the cavern and became a hymn of salvation. Vibration thrilled the air; everything was shaking. From the roof came dust and crumbling, cracks opened and rocks began tumbling. The rolling stones sang, and their song threw Nehushtan from confusion into madness. I gave the rock one final stroke and made my move, diving under her belly and doubling back toward the egress. By the time she realised I was no longer present, it was too late, the roof collapsed, and the serpent was trapped; her evil buried under a mountain of elemental delight.

The sprint to the surface was faster than the journey down. I succeeded in reaching the cave's entrance only to discover it closed. Vacillating, self-doubt found me looking back; perhaps I had mistakenly spurred from the main tunnel; perhaps I was a faltering fool whose steps needed retracing. As I turned, the direct lustre of my sword was withdrawn, revealing the wall I had been staring at was in fact translucent. I had not been mistaken at all, the entrance stood before me, its opening sealed by Nehushtan's thick web; this was her trapdoor, and I her prisoner.

Deep in the earth's recesses, the dark queen remained, weighed down, buried under glimmering stone where her power and poison would diminish and eventually evaporate. However, that was unknown to me; I was still caught up in the flight and imagined her to be boiling toward the surface. I attacked the webbing frenetically until a tear was made, enough to squeeze my body through.

I hastened around the cavern's perimeter, my flight from fear metamorphosing into intense desire for freedom. Eventually, I forgot that I was running from anything, I was running for my life.

Circumnavigation, though arduous, was uneventful. On occasion I spied a worm blindly searching for food. Fatigue, which almost claimed me in the tunnel, had passed, and, in its place, resolve steeled my heart. Arriving at the next flight of stairs, I climbed, encouraging myself that thus far all was well, and hoped these steps would transport me to my goal. Halfway ascending, weariness returned with a vengeance. So, in the peace that always accompanies true courage, I withdrew from sight as best I could and allowed myself some necessary rest.

CHAPTER 14

Mutatis Mutandis

I slept my way into a second dream wherein I sat upon a spacious green under the warming sun. Trees were raining apple blossom, white petals showering and dancing in the balmy breeze. Before me a young boy, barely five years old, was engrossed in the joy of play. Momentarily, he looked at me and smiled through innocent eyes, then continued his game. That smile touched the innermost part of me; it made me want to laugh and cry, to leave behind my hard, meaningless torments, to wrap my arms around him and find atonement in my heart.

"Son, what is your name?" My voice sounded harsh and cold as the stone upon which I slept.

He answered with astonishing gravity, "I am *The Unforgettable*," the smile remaining in his eyes, "I am the one whose name you have forgotten."

I stepped forwards: Immediately a crevice opened at my feet swallowing all manner of creation that dwelt on the verge of existence, a bottomless pit threatening to drag me in. Gravity sucked me down. However, at that precise moment of my plummeting I heard the roar of an enormous lion which propelled me backwards with such force that I rolled several times before thudding into a huge door.

"You are far too heavy to cross The Void," the boy sang, "Much sorrow you have, too many burdens; they are all heading towards the abyss and will drag you down with them."

The boy continued his explanation, "Between us lies a vast and impenetrable ocean of grief. Down there," he motioned, "is where all you have become belongs; but it is not your destiny. Ultimately you will find yourself with me."

Irritation trickled into my voice, "I am what I am!" And then, after some thought, I resigned, "Actually, I am nothing; I do not even have a name."

"It is fear of being nothing that provokes your anger against me;" the boy returned, "your self-contempt! Truly, if you were nothing you would not be able to say 'I,' you would have to say, 'Not I.' Further, it takes something to say nothing. So, you see, even nothing can be something. Soon you will understand. Now, I have a gift for you." He bounded across the open chasm as surely as if he were walking on solid ground, and placed into my hand a light, brilliant and dazzling, so bright my eyes could not force a look. "This is Nepsis, the fixed star by which all things can be judged. Keep her before you, and your course will stay true. Now your sword, if I may?"

Reluctantly I parted with the shadow-slayer. The boy took hold and flayed it around; with giggles and whoops he fought an imaginary army. "You have dealt old Nehushtan a deathly blow!" He chirped. "Now, greater shall be your mighty glow!" Then he threw my sword in the air and Nepsis followed. In an explosion of light, the star aligned with the sword. I caught it as it fell. Nepsis was affixed to the hilt. The boy smiled again, and returned to his game. The dream ended, and with it, my rest.

The stairs were a dangerous climb, increasingly precipitous, worn smooth through overuse, and covered with black greasy slime. I soon realised these stairs were not constructed for the purpose of ascending, but descending; to rise upon them was to go against their nature and necessitated enormous exertion. Slipping and sliding, clutching and scrambling, I tackled the perilous slope until I reached the post and pulled myself over the ledge.

Hanging before me were colossal doors many times my height; an inscription on the threshold read:

THE LABYRINTH OF MUTATIS MUTANDIS
Come One - Come All

The great doors opened with an ease that belied their size, and I entered an enormous hall with numerous doors left and right. Walking the length of the corridor, I tested each handle. None responded until at the hall's extremity a narrow door allowed admittance. It was an alarming entrance, for the room was crowded with people, all looking at me, every person identical; Every person was me. An eternity had lapsed since I had seen that face.

Through the room I walked, the crowd following without drawing near. That was when I realised the room was replete with mirrors. Closer inspection revealed the reflections, though my own, were not as identical as first perceived. Flaws in each mirror made variable distortions, some more obvious than others. First sight of me drew much fascination, for I was unaccustomed to my appearance. The attraction, however, did not last and soon I was aware of all the blemishes and defects and imperfections of my mistaken identity, each enhanced by the varying flaws in the mirrors. Making my way through to the other side became a dismal, depressing walk amidst fallen images. I was in a maze of mirrors, sick at the sight of myself, and without a clue how I could get out. I was lost with only my miserable imperfection for company.

Slumping down, I buried my head in my hands, and leaned back against my mirrored reflection only to somersault back through the mirror into night. Impenetrable blackness! I groped along the walls of a narrow, claustrophobic duct towards slips of sharp rectangular light that cut into the darkness not too far ahead. Upon reaching the luminous shafts I padded the area, grasped a circular knob, twisted, opened, and discovered I was back in the entrance hall.

With a solid clunk, the door closed behind. I tried opening it again, but only one door in this corridor responded, the door *into* the maze of mirrors. Again, I found myself facing myself a thousand times over. This time I deliberately pushed against the first mirror encountered and walked into its dark passageway. Once again it led me to the great hall of unamenable doors.

Presentiment gave me assurance that one of the mirrors would prove itself the egress out of the castle. So, I began to work my way systematically through all the mirrored gateways, passing through one, and then another, keeping close account of mirrors already appraised. Each traversing took me through dark passages, some longer than others, but each invariably returned me to the castle entrance. I passed through hundreds of mirrors; not one directed anywhere substantial.

At length, and in frustration, I retreated to the exterior of the labyrinth, preferring isolation to a room full of me. Staring at the threshold inscription, I sat, quiet, confused, and despondent: 'So, this is how I fell to the nether regions.' I surmised, 'Through chasing image and illusion. *Mutatis mutandis*, in despair I could go no other way but down.' Heavy of heart, I bowed my head and closed my eyes.

Whether in dream, or vision, or reality, I do not know, but I caught the fresh fragrance of apple, and looking I saw the boy, *The Unforgettable*, playing on the green. He signalled me to approach. So, I started toward him, but walked barely five paces before the ground at my feet fell into chasm. Again, I was saved from falling by a roar that sent me sprawling backwards in the process. He smiled, "You are still too old and heavy. Why are you here?"

"I have been trying to find a way through the castle, but I fear there is none."

"The Labyrinth is an enigma. It would be especially complicated for one such as you."

"Please do not mock me," I retorted petulantly, "Is there any way through the maze?"

"There is no way as long as all the reflections remain; the interior castle needs simplification. You are the maker of those mirrors and you alone can unmake them. There is one reflection true to your nature; through that you must go; but you will never choose that door while others remain, they will always lead you away from the upward path. Strike the mirrors and nullify your distortions, until you discover your true image. That is the way out of here." I arose with renewed determination to once again find myself in the labyrinth. "Wait!" The boy spoke with uncommon urgency, "It is a perilous thing to tear down an image. Many have grown so attached that they are destroyed with the destruction. Much anguish awaits you in there, but it is only to the hopeless that hope bears strength. So, remember this: Misery and affliction, perceived through the demolition of your false selves, are not enduring, for they are not attached to Reality."

"Already I despair, for how, when I have such little memory of my visage, can I tell the true from the false?"

"That is why I gave you Nepsis. Her light is unmoving and will guide wherever certainty wavers. Do not be hasty with the mirrors! Cherish the mirror of truth! Should you destroy the true, you will be lost forever."

I motioned to move back to the castle when the boy spoke again, "Before you go, I have one more thing to give you. It is a parchment. Don't bother reading it, the message will mean nothing to you now. I do not even know what is written upon it, nor do I care to look, for it is not for me. It is a sign and signs are for those who are travelling somewhere. I have arrived. There may come a time when you will find it useful."

As I was folding the parchment into my belt the boy faded and left me staring at The Labyrinth's portico. I was soon reflecting on the reflection before me. It was definitely me, but, as I gave to it my complete attention, the mirror unfolded its peculiarity. There was vanity within this stature which became more apparent, when, from the figure's shadow came forth a crowd of others. They were not the reflection yet they reflected in every way my reflection's style, philosophy, and modus operandi. The company of aficionados were made in his image, fashioned according to his design, and he delighted in their similitude, and they delighted in his pleasure. Was this really me? Full of hubris? Content as long as attention remains fixed upon me? As long as people agree with me? And applaud me? Enjoying others inasmuch as they enjoy me? Laughing because I loved making people laugh with me? Living to see myself reinvented in the lives of others? Selecting others according to their ability to fulfil my ideal? Creating an order, a church, a following, a legacy, a dynasty? This reflection was not fully human, it did not allow for the existence of others: It should be broken! Yet when it came to the task, I was loath to destroy; I enjoyed what I saw. This guru was a likeable leader, he was undoubtedly charismatic, yet all that is no excuse for the absorption of others into one's personality, certainly, it is not enough to make one a man. Surely, the continuance of this theatre would ruin my chance of escaping the maze. Such a shroud would simply ensure my slide back into the pit would bear company. Stringent honesty demanded a negative verdict. Harnessing all the powers of my will, and with such a violent struggle that I shook to the bone, I cracked the looking glass and watched me break into a thousand tiny pieces at my feet.

As I looked further, behold a reflection sniggered, an embarrassed, insincere, insecure titter. At once I thought, 'There may have been a time when insincerity and insecurity married themselves within my heart, but I have been where they take me and felt the emptiness that lies therein. The clever know-it-all's, who know enough of themselves to distrust all others, never know others well enough to entrust themselves and thereby discover their true self. To live without substantiation, to live with that sarcastic jibe in my heart; that is not the life for me.' And the second mirror cracked.

Another, I smashed, who came to the fore applauding people and things but never loving them. I esteemed them because I had reason to esteem, but love requires no reasons; this one was all head and no heart.

A further reflection before my eyes came enlarged and engorged; he was the supreme materialist. He stood, a solitary figure, happy with his own applause, unhappy with anyone else's; dull, and bored with anything but himself, unable to laugh and smile except at the expense of others; this figure was intimidating to child and adult alike. Yet, I stood before him transfixed, somehow admiring his independence, his cold audacity, his narrow determinism. As I did, rigidity stole into my veins making me hard and severe. I observed my reflection in the mirror begin to assume the cold hues of granite as surely as if I'd beheld Medusa's head. Before apoplexy paralysed the last vestiges of life within, I struck the hideous model and felt the cold weight leave my heart.

The mirrors, by and large, were all variations of these: a multitude of self-made men who made themselves nothing but thought they were something. Most willingly divulged their secrets as I gave them scrutiny, for after all they were me, *mutatis mutandis*, or at least they found their source in me, and seeing themselves in me they deliberated that I was what they were. They were wrong! Accordingly, I went throughout the room smashing and cracking, shattering and breaking, with hilt of sword and fist. The more I smashed, the more committed I became. The boy was right, however, each breaking had its pain, as if I was abusing myself. But like a warrior in battle, pain became my food, and I demolished all visages that through excess or absence were clearly not my own.

Broken mirrors amassed till eventually I found myself wading through and climbing over mountains of glass. Dissimilarity from the plumb-line of nobility, humility, and grace lay in piles across the floor. Several mirrors remained untested: I stood before each for a long season pondering their resemblance, searching for distinction; but I failed with both eyes and heart to discern flaw or shadow, I was deadlocked! I dare not shatter another for fear of destroying the mirror of truth - Stalemate! I knew not what to do. I wished to return to the castle entrance and find the boy again, but leaving the room would not ensure finding him, and who knows, by some sardonic magic it might mean the resurrection of the crowd, "Aaghh! Curse this disparity!"

Hope abandoned my heart to despair. But then, through dark and threatening clouds, the memory of Nepsis shone. Quickly I reached for my sword, and learned there is more reality in dreams than most are prepared to believe, for set in the golden hilt was a large crystal pulsating with all the pleasure of a friendly star. I set her before my eyes and shortly the stone began to glow and grow, surrounding me with light, until I saw, not merely from without as one sees by torch or light of day, but also from within; the light radiated without and within. Vision altered, and with it a subtle anomaly appeared in the looking glass before me: In the image's eye there winked a scepticism, as if everything had a catch. The sceptical intent was not that my reflection gave no place to The Most-High, but rather gave too much. The glass figure believed very much in The One but left no room for man; man was a joke to tickle one's fancy, a marionette, God's plaything. My reflection harboured a terrible theism that imagines nothing but deity, denying altogether the outlines of human personality and will. I had not scepticism of God, but of man. In that wink, I knew this could not be me, for my life and the lives of others were no trifling matter. The glass shattered at my feet and I moved on.

Coming upon another, I again employed Nepsis' rule. Her brilliance was cast, and through her light I could detect a faint shadow hidden in the crevices of the face. The shadow was evasive, withdrawing into the very pores of my image's skin. However, Nepsis gave the image no relief and finally the shadow submitted to her authority. This reflection walked close to the truth but there were secrets he wished to keep, preferring to hide and pretend than have an open heart and singular face. Feelings of vulnerability became acute: What if everyone could read me like an open book? Terror! What if all my thoughts were laid bare, and the secrets of my heart became obvious to all and sundry? Horror! What about my motives? What if they should be exposed? I do not even know why I do the things I do. What if even the good that I do is to satisfy my own ego? Such is the case for any who live with shadow in their lives; they give place to overwhelming fear. All must come into the light otherwise we sentence ourselves to eternal twilight. For as surely as oxygen enters our lungs, whatever is in us is truly what we are in. I smashed through my terror; for there is not enough room in the heart of a true man to contain even an ounce of fear. Glass scattered all over the ground.

Next came a face that exuded the calm confidence of spiritual mysticism. He imparted a sense of peace, as though he had arrived at the secret of the universe. His serenity created an alluring intrigue concerning his mystical assurance. Yet this face, upon facing the terror of Nepsis, began to lose its composure. So far did its features fall away from each other that the man in the moon had more of a face than this man in the mirror. This face escaped me. One ear drew so far away from the other that it was no longer an ear but a landscape; the nose grew so large that it was impossible to see anything else; it had to be thought of all on its own. It made me doubt whether there is any such thing as a face, or whether there is anything firm and secure at all. This person had not a belief, not a creed, not a faith in God, himself, anyone, or anything, this image was a living doubt, an unbelief; he believed in nothing; not as the nihilist who doesn't believe in *anything*, but as the solipsist who literally believes in nothing. This mirror had to go.

Three down, three to go. The next mirror held two simple but elegant features: the face was pure and undisturbed. Though I tested it with the fixed star, it was absent of shadow and suspicion, exuding harmony and tranquillity. The face also featured innocence, barely perceptible, yet utterly present. Here, I recognised a glimmer of *The Unforgettable*. Convinced this was the true mirror, in my excitement I pushed against it. I looked and saw a corridor, not as dark and dismal as those previously traversed, but two long silhouettes crossed its walls. Instantly I halted. The boy cautioned that no other image could remain, and there were yet two unexamined doors of glass. 'Freedom will not avail itself where false images abide,' said he. I stepped back, every impulse urging me to smash the two remaining mirrors and be done with it. However, they had not been tested, and wisdom would first judge their authenticity or lack thereof. I had not come this far to be undone by impatience.

Advancing, with Nepsis ascending, I beheld a man, no, more than a man, a warrior, a hero, a super-man. Impressive! Instantly, I rejoiced that patience had staid my hand. I wanted this to be me. I wanted to be more than a man, I wanted to be the hero, the warrior, the champion. Returning the gaze, it was obvious the image was pleased that I was pleased. That was his undoing; for I realised a true hero would take little pleasure in impressing another, especially if that other was himself. Nepsis revealed to me that above all others this one wanted to be *thought* important. Success, piety, vigils, righteous and heroic acts, and every noble manner were pursued with relentless energy; believing in himself; saving the world without ever realising he was striving to save himself. He took great pleasure in rescuing damsels and slaying dragons purely because these acts pleasured the phantom and fantasy that filled his mind. With a single blow I put him out of his malignant misery.

One remaining mirror required analysis. In there I saw standing, tall but unobtrusive, strong yet contrite, active though tranquil, a saint. I must admit, even with the light of Nepsis he seemed flawless. He was as impressive in humility as he was in bravery. He gained no delight from my attention. A gold band, slender and simple, wove round his head like a halo, and the tunic he wore emblazoned a large golden cross. Of all mirrors, this was the first in which I had noticed the tunic. I looked at my clothes and could see that I also wore the tunic except mine was ragged and filthy, mere threads bedraggling an emaciated torso. I returned to the reflection; the cross descended almost to the ground; and there I was taken aback, for I saw that the image was wearing boots, which I thought strange because I was not. I spoke to my reflection, "The place where you are standing is holy ground, take off your shoes." Without reluctance he removed his boots, and there I saw, threading the length of his feet, blue veins oozing yellow puss. He was exposed. His roots were rotten, his nobility a façade, his integrity was found wanting. Oblivious, his countenance suggested no recognition whatsoever. Religious deception is the most insidious fraud any man can swallow. Of all the mirrors, none tore my soul like the destruction of this one.

Innocence faced me in the sole remaining mirror. I took a deep breath and pressed my hand to it. Instead of darkness, a flood of light greeted me. A hallway of reflective glass led me to an ivory staircase. The innocent impression of *The Unforgetable* walking alongside until I reached the summit and entered *The Great Expanse*: And it was a sight to behold.

CHAPTER 15

The Great Expanse

Incandescent fields of gold and green stretched as far as the eye could see; rivers, streams, and waterfalls were flanked by tropical verdure; snow-capped mountains rimmed a hazy horizon; an unchained menagerie of flamingo and gazelle, toucan and tiger, robin and unicorn, to name a few, were flying, and singing, and playing, and laying in the sun; clouds, here, white and wispy, there, bulging and precipitous, with unbroken rainbows crowning the symphony before me. I had walked into paradise, and here I would remain, forever content.

Days drifted into seasons in my wonderland. All past trials and pain became a distant memory. However, with the passage of time, an unconscious restlessness was born; an embryonic longing that grew into a great yawning hole which yearned for some other. Entering this consummate perfection instantly induced unequivocal delight; remaining here eventually found me doubly forsaken. I needed someone; it mattered little if they were friend or foe; I just wanted someone with whom I might share this paragon of beauty. Despairingly, it was not to be, nor could it ever be, for this world was of my own design; a vision splendid, where all is befitting me, and unfit for another.

In my desire for that other, I began to lose hold of myself. I walked the fields day after day, week after week, with the grass as my bed and the naked sky for a covering, dispiriting all I saw into a progressively desolate and lonely state. My mind was fixed upon a solitary plea for companionship.

Demands unfulfilled, invariably develop into anger, and then despair: I was despairing on the day I woke to change. Birds were singing, their communal songs mocking my isolation; but in the morning light my eyes were brightened by the most beautiful sight: A woman swimming in my river. Her arms gracefully stroking the surface, her long legs dancing beneath: Here swam the answer to my prayers. Now is come completion, now there is need for nothing more. In a singular moment paradise returned, and my happiness ran over. With her I could run forever.

The object of my desire made that pool wherein she bathed an ocean of love. Her eyes found mine transfixed; they revealed no surprise, no shame, no displeasure. I beckoned her to me and asked her name. She emerged shimmering, "I am known by many names. I will answer to the name you have in your heart for me."

"I will call you Eve," I lied! For in my heart, I knew her name to be *Lilith*. However, I had always liked the name Eve, and it seemed much more appropriate in this Eden of mine. Eve knew I lied and cared not. I gave her all my attention and she was content with that. How could I do otherwise? Her unblemished beauty opened my eyes and blinded me to all else.

In my blindness, I saw not with each day's passing the beauty of the great expanse fading, and the wonderland fast becoming a desert. Temperatures soared, though I did not heed it. Until one afternoon of exceptional scorching, my parched tongue demanded satisfaction. With anticipation I approached the soothing waters of my river.

"Stay, my love," Eve urged, "Stay here, while I fetch whatever you desire." Thirst made me deaf to her plea. Reaching the river-bank, my legs buckled; I was stunned by what was before my eyes. My river was dry. Scales fell from my eyes as I surveyed paradise lost: golden fields turned to chaff, lush vegetation withered, mountains, clouds, and rainbows, all were gone, animals and birds lay dead on the sun-scorched ground.

"Eve," I gasped. She turned, and facing me, stole my heart. Momentarily I surrendered sadness, forgot the stark, arid agony surrounding, and satiated my primal urge with her splendour. Then thirst, as yet unsatisfied, forced me to reiterate, "What happened to the river? What happened to paradise, my love?"

Eve was eating an apple; a dry withered thing that perched inappropriately against her perfect lips, "Do not fret over such things my love; it is merely the passing of seasons."

"Do you know when this season will end? We will not survive long in this place."

"That, I cannot say, but pass it will. Everything changes here, everything except for me. I will remain. I am your heart's desire."

She allowed the apple to fall from her fingers and walked slowly, rhythmically toward me, every step a lesson in delight. Lacing her fingers into mine, I was led to a lonely pool like a lamb to the slaughter. Bending low, Eve lifted water to my mouth, "Now drink from my hand." It drizzled through her fingers onto my tongue and down my throat. Repeating the motion, she poured until I was quenched.

"What about you, my precious wonder?" I reciprocated, "Won't you drink?"

"I have no need. It is sufficient for me that you are satisfied."

Though Eve continued to occupy my thoughts, doubt and question had entered my mind: Doubting my purpose, questioning Eve's. Eventually suspicion ran unhindered, and in due course, Eve's seething beauty and sultry voice were not enough to hide reality. As the remaining pool of my river dried, I asked if she knew where we might find sustenance.

"If you go," she answered, "you must leave me behind, for I am bound to this place: I am *The Desert.*"

Urgency escalated, "We must go, or we will surely die!"

"I do not know what it means to die, but if we do, we die together."

I was torn: To remain, would mean certain death; but leaving Eve would also be a death. I held her hand and sighed her name, "Lilith."

Where that word originated, I do not know, for Eve had been the only name on my lips since our first meeting. But with its utterance I saw beauty grow cold.

"Lilith, what's wrong?"

All colour drained from her face; her eyes were aghast; a trill noise emanated from her throat.

"Lilith, my love, you need water. Come, drink the little we have."

Her eyes locked onto mine, and, with helpless appellation, she spoke her final words, "I have to go now. You will find assistance in the house on the edge of this land."

Her face and body dehydrated; Eve shrivelled, until, like the desert, she turned to dust and was blown away by the wind.

Life faded before my very eyes, my life! I was left with nothing, no-one, nowhere. Would that I had never known paradise. Would that I had never met Eve, never touched her skin, or heard her voice, never tasted love, if love it was. Where in this emptiness is there solace for the heart that deceives itself? I was gutted with awful futility, excruciating betrayal. The overwhelming anarchy within pushed and shoved my mind and heart to come to terms with what had been found and lost.

The questions were blown back into my face by the desert wind and remained unanswered.

CHAPTER 16

Phantasmagoria

I wandered the dry desert with the four winds kicking sand in my face, till there was as much desert within as without. Strange as this sounds, and though at first, I could not swallow it, the arid desert was my salvation. The reprisal of pain, the raking thirst, blistering sunburn, blazing feet and smouldering head performed their task to perfection, forcing me yet again to face reality. It was an accumulating reality; layer upon layer. I came to my senses, and remembered my reason for being, at least my reason for being there: I was there to get out! I must find the door out of this netherworld. I knew not which direction to take, but, when my eyes lifted from despondency, before me a star rose brightly and beckoned me forward.

I clawed up and rolled down many a dune, until one lone night I beheld far, far away, a house sitting peacefully under the summoning star. As I gave it my distant attention, a bright and sudden flash emanated from inside the building. It came as a lightning bolt, followed shortly by the brief silhouette of a solitary figure wandering from the building and disappearing over one of the desert dunes.

Before too long I was rapping on the door. As there was no answer, I tentatively entered. Respite from the harsh conditions was immediate. It was a simple home, a solitary room, a solitary table, a solitary chair, a solitary window on the same wall as the solitary door, and a solitary bed in the corner. A simple meal invited me to the table: bread, cheese, and a jug of water. I ate and drank, and was content. Then, I slept the night, or possibly several nights, away.

Waking, the table was again set with the same simple fare, and I sat to my second meal. Eating passed into pondering: How did the food arrive? Who might the patron of this refuge be? As though lured by my thoughts, an old man, short and sinewy in stature, entered the house, wearing a mischievous face with large eyes and profoundly rounded cheeks. Immediately, he made much fuss over my waking. I was attempting an apology for intruding without invitation, but he would hear nothing of it.

"Welcome to my home, The Hankering House, I like to call it." He didn't really talk, rather, he babbled. "I have been expecting you."

He gave a toothsome smile, and bowed such an exaggerated gesture, it made me question, "How could you have been expecting me? I had neither direction nor invitation to this place. If it wasn't for the star, I would never have come."

The old man frowned, "What star? I know nothing of any star."

"Well, I have been following a star for several days and nights, and it led me here."

"I'll hear no more mention of stars, thank you very much. You're not going to get very far here if you keep looking up." He fussed at the fireplace mumbling, "There be millions of stars in the desert - *millions!* And, What's he mean by a star over my house?"

"Then answer me," I questioned, "If I wasn't led here by a star, how could you have been expecting me?"

"Of course, I was expecting you. Everyone in search of paradise comes here."

"Paradise?" I quizzed. "I've seen what you might call paradise, and I want nothing more of that heartless utopia."

Ignoring my standpoint, the old man's eyebrows lifted and he adopted a benevolent attitude, "I am The Candyman. It is through me that people's dreams come true. Don't worry, we'll turn your desert into paradise in no time at all."

"No thank you. Leave the desert as it is. I am looking for the way out."

Having exhausted conversation, he returned to the door and gave a resigned, "We'll see about that!" His face was a mixture of amusement and question, his voice, an amalgam of cynicism and bewilderment. No sooner had he disappeared than I finished all the food on the table.

Shortly after my meal, the old man returned, attended by an associate. The companion was wearing a mantle, the colour of wine, which veiled the face in shadow.

"Have you enjoyed your meal?" hummed the old man, his eyes bobbling on top of his head, "I do hope so. There is much to be done. Paradise awaits."

"Not interested!" I objected. "I'm not looking for paradise."

"Now, now, let's hear nothing more of that. Everybody wants paradise, and I'm here to provide it."

"Not me! Not now! Never again!"

"Well, I think you will change your mind." The Candyman's face evolved mischievous. He reached toward his companion and removed the mantle. It was Eve, resurrected.

"I found her not far from here. Most beautiful, is she not? Her name is *Fata Morgana*, and I believe she is yours."

I beheld her beauty, and thought it cold. This time ardour would not get the better of me. The fire within had burned itself out, "This is not for me! I am leaving!"

"Fine, come with us." They moved toward the door.

"No! Through that door, I entered. I want the door out, not the door in."

Colour drained from The Candyman's face, and it took some time before he spoke again; rasping in a shallow and incredulous tone, "No-one ever enters this house through that door excepting myself and the master. That door leads to paradise; from paradise it is but a short journey through sinking sands to the netherworld, *Hell*, I tell you! From where no man returns."

"I have come from hell, and paradise became hell to me. So, I want my leave, but I will not be taking your door." My voice was becoming bolder, "There is nothing out there for me."

The atmosphere grew menacing. My fingers were not far from my sword. "Tell me," I pressed, "If that is the way out, and not the way in, by which entrance come your regular guests?"

After a brief pause, he motioned flippantly, "They all fall through the roof. I'm forever patching it to keep everything looking right."

I leaped from floor to table, then to rafter, slashing with my sword at the thatch roof and producing a sizeable hole. Heat from the desert sun was the sole result. There was no door, only a cloudless sky.

"You are lying." I charged as I dropped to the ground.

The old man could not hide his derision. I brought the sword's point to his throat. Blood oozed a trail down his neck. But he would not divulge house secrets.

I surveyed the room. There were no other doors or windows. So, I set to other possibilities: pulling up the bed, rummaging through cupboards, turning over chair and table. Throughout my searching the old man was chirping, "Cold; cold; very cold. There is only one door here, and that is the door out, or in, depending on your perspective. Out of the house, and in to paradise."

I sat on the chair, with The Candyman looking far too pleased at my frustration, and rested my head against the sword's hilt. Nepsis was glowing, and she introduced a thought, 'A star brought me here, perhaps a star will show me the way out; perhaps, once again, Nepsis will reveal what my eyes cannot see.'

Eve discerned my thoughts and attempted distraction, "My love, let me pour some wine for you to soothe your mood and wipe the lines from your face."

I felt the power of her will, but my intent was unwavering. I raised the sword's hilt level with my eyes. Nepsis' light grew bright, searching the room, penetrating every nook. "There!" The wall across from the table disclosed The Candyman's secret. Tracing into it was the outline of a door, a thick heavy door, hinged in such a way that I would have to pull it open. There was no handle, so I felt around its rough edge seeking a finger-hold.

"Dorranor."

That name? The dungeons had worn out the memory. I could not recall when last I'd heard it. Some interior emptiness within me answered the call, and it froze me instantly.

Eve, it was, who spoke. She spoke the name a second time, "Dorranor."

My hands fell limp.

Pleased with herself and the effect of her naming, Eve called again. This time my knees folded under and I slumped to the floor.

The Candyman began jumping around the room, cackling and chortling and whooping, fondling Eve's hand, pointing, and tumbling, leaping on the table, swinging from the rafter; He'd turned monkey.

I lay prostrate; immobilised, paralysed. Eve looked down contemptuously. She was laughing. I had never heard her laugh before and found it a strange laugh, unlike a woman unlike a man; her laughter was hollow, hollow as the darkness into which I felt myself sinking. Then, like the dry reach of a sick empty stomach, the name erupted from memory's pit, "Chemosh!" I denounced.

"So, Dorran! Finally, you recognise your old friend. Have I dressed to please? Am I acceptable in the guise of your beautiful Eve?" The scorn in his voice was building, "Or was her name Lilith? Of course, your pleasure is no longer relevant; not now that you have so calmly and willingly bowed before me." He laughed, long and vacuous.

Deception! I had been duped again. But this one thing was for me, I had pierced his disguise, and my mind had clarity. 'Eve was a lie!' I realised, 'If she was a lie, then all is a lie; and if all is a lie, this paralysing weakness may not be the stronghold it appears.' I began to search for another strength, a deeper strength.

Chemosh lined Eve's face with burlesque derision, "Dorran, fallen prince of the free, what a merry little chase you have given me. Did you think you could actually leave my kingdom? *Nobody leaves!*"

He bent down and pushed his face close to mine, saliva drooling and spitting over me as he pressed his point, "We will help you remember what it is to suffer for your crime. The lady of the cavern, the winged one, wishes to renew her acquaintance with you." He laughed again, "Yes, Dorranor. We've all missed you."

I had not been called by any name in ten lifetimes. Now, in the space of minutes, Chemosh had called me two. Was I Dorran or Dorranor? Just as the same name can sound sweetly sung when spoken by a friend, yet toxic on the lips an enemy, I concluded that if either was truly my name, I am nothing that Chemosh would seek to call me. Reaching deep within my soul, I fought against weakened flesh, and found hidden strength. I struggled to my feet, looked Chemosh in the eye, and it was my turn to laugh; But not just yet. I would reserve celebration until liberty became reality.

Chemosh, choking on his rancid breath, was flushed with panic. He called out, "Dorranor," but the name fell like lead to the floor. Revulsion filled my heart and I wrapped my hand around Eve's throat. The Candyman leaped upon me and began hitting, and kicking, and biting. I let go my hold of Chemosh and pulled the monkey off my back. He rolled over the floor, but I was quick and split his head with my sword. I returned to The Ugly still masquerading in Eve's false beauty. Perhaps that is what saved him; perhaps that is what saved me?

For instead of delivering a fatal blow, I thrust my sword through his shoulder, sticking him to the doorpost. Then I turned to take my leave.

I felt round the perimeter of the secret door and discovered a place where I could squeeze the tips of my fingers. Suction fought against me; the door was stuck solid; immovable!

Raising an intense shrill, Chemosh spluttered, "That door cannot be opened from this side, you fool. Gravity withstands you. I told you; *nobody* leaves this world!"

"Well, I am leaving!" I insisted, "You can rot in hell without me, Chemosh!"

The sword's light was burning bright, and where it pierced, Chemosh's skin was smouldering. Nepsis had been busy disrobing every facet of the mask, and Eve's beauty was melting away. However, I could not tell if Chemosh was discomforted or disturbed, for he pulled himself together and spoke again, the shrill note evaporated, his voice mellowed and developed a persuasive, mesmerising posture, "Why do you call me Chemosh? Why call me by that name? My name is Dorran-ap-Lusdburn. You are Dorranor; I am your friend, your father. I have looked after you for more years than I can remember, and I would look after you many more, in spite of how you have treated me."

I continued prying the door.

"Why leave? What do you think you will find out there? It's a fearful thing to step through that door. Why would you leave something of your own making? You would not have made this world were the outside better. There is nothing out there but wandering, and loneliness, and the harsh cruelty of feigned and forgotten friendship. Here is home. Your home is here, with me!"

I should not have listened, for confusion's hand was creeping over my mind. I was becoming light headed and heavy hearted.

When I turned to answer, by some dark magic the house had changed. I now looked upon an expansive room with fine furniture, ornate tapestries, elegant rugs, and a large warm fireplace. A man was walking slowly toward me, a fatherly figure with greying hair, well dressed, smiling a knowing, concerned smile. He spoke without deference, "Come now, cease your striving and let us talk awhile. Do not think for a moment that I want anything other than what is best for you. I am wanting what you are wanting. A share in the life designed for you, your destiny. That way," motioning his hand toward the invisible door as though dismissing the universe, "The way you were heading, is the way of pain, unimaginable pain and heartache. It is that which brought you to me in the first place. It is pain I am trying to prevent. For return to me you shall, once you discover I am speaking truth."

Dangerous words, warm words like mead, lulled and dulled my senses, persuading me to doubt myself. In that valley, where there is no telling what is truth, my hands fumbled, searching for something, anything, to cling to. And in my belt my fumbling fingers felt a parchment.

"It is most common," Dorran-ap-Lusdburn continued, "for the young to convince themselves they are hard done by. But you would be a cruel child to accuse me of treating you badly. Why look, everything you have ever wanted is right here."

I fought the spell of his voice, drew out the parchment and began unravelling.

"What is that you have there, my son?"

I gave no reply.

He continued, "And of course, grass is often assumed greener on the other side, but it was for greener grass that you ventured here. The only green you have is what you make for yourself in paradise. Out there, life has little colour; all is dull, dull, *Dull* I tell you."

I unrolled the scroll. There were few words upon it, but they were powerful and timely:

> BEWARE THE ILLUSION
> OF THE UNBRIDLED HEART
> WHERE WILD IMAGINATION
> TAMED BY THE BARREN WORD
> FALLS AGAIN IN VAIN DECEPTION
> AND TURNS FROM THE CHOSEN PATH

"What is that in your hand Dorranor? Give it to me."

I handed over the parchment. A great struggle was unleashed around me. The old house with its simple, sterile interior was fighting to return in spasms of fluctuating, pulsatory visibility.

With a glance, Dorran-ap-Lusdburn dismissed the small scroll, "As I thought, foolish propaganda from those who know just enough to be dangerous, and not enough to do anything of merit. Meaningless words create all the confusion in this world."

For a moment I lost sight of it. Then, with a condescending grin, he handed the parchment back to me.

"What do you think you will find when you walk out that door?"

The atmospheric struggle calmed; the milieu resumed its stately elegance.

"What do you want? Freedom? You have all the freedom you could possibly wish for right here. You even have the freedom to walk out that door; Though I do not advise it. Walk out if you want; walk in and out at your leisure. But do not think that once you are out you can return to what you had. You may never be able to conjure your paradise again. So, my son, it is clear as can be; the freedom is in here, not out there."

His argument was strong, and I could find no reply. Looking again at the parchment in my hands, I lurched into confusion, for it had changed. Instead of warning, it showed a picture, a reproduction of the room in which we were conversing: furniture, tapestries, inviting fireplace, rugs, a caged canary in the corner, and a plaque on the wall reading *Home Is Where The Heart Is*. I did not remember seeing that, but looking up at the wall, sure enough, there was the sign. It was hanging a little off centre. I wondered how I could have missed seeing those words that suggested such strange comfort.

"A picture is always worth a thousand words!" He smiled broadly as he perceived his effect upon my mind. His grin seemed to expand and fill the room, "I have a name for that door you were trying to open: I call it The Door of Fools, Fools Door. Dorranor, get a grip on reality; the stuff you can see and feel. Your thoughts of emancipation are an illusion, dreams for a fool. And you are no fool Dorranor."

"Illusion?" I pondered. "I am sure the parchment said something about: Beware the Illusion."

"Yes, that's right! Beware the illusion of freedom; the ingrained futility and deception underlying all the false assumptions of your mind." Dorran-ap-Lusdburn was advancing in confidence, his countenance brimming with arrogance, "What if freedom is not what you think it is? What if it is not all warm and comforting like an open fireplace, and cool and refreshing as clear running water? If it is warmth you want, we have a fireplace that's been burning for an eternity. Also, there is no such thing as refreshing; nothing, old or new, is fresh anymore, my son." His voice assumed an air of indignant reasonableness, "Freedom is just a word; an overused, underexposed word. It is not all that you wish it to be."

He fixed one eye on the birdcage. The canary grew agitated, "Look at what happens when I take out this bird." He opened the cage, grabbed the bird rather roughly, and threw it up in the air. Tiny wings thrashed feverishly, until, regaining its bearings, the canary promptly flew back behind bars. "You see? Even a bird knows where it belongs."

I drew little consolation from his demonstration, "So, you would make me a caged bird? Your prisoner?"

An unpleasant storm rapidly descended upon Dorran-ap-Lusdburn's face, "Do not insult me or the house of your abode these numberless years by suggesting I am some jailer. Your warped perception muddles your mind and perverts all vain notions freedom. What if freedom is naked nothingness? What if freedom is the terror of nihil? Annihilation! What if freedom is the lone and affectionless state? For I tell you, freedom can be nothing more! Should you meet just one other person, you will be held responsible and accountable for and to them, and therein forsake yourself and your precious quest for freedom."

I opened my mouth, but no words came.

"Dorranor, Dorranor, Dorranor!" He was looking smug. "You have always been the impetuous one; always the idealist; never the pragmatist. This is just another one of your many flights of fancy, and it is no joyful ride, but one that will bring you crashing down to earth with a thud. There would be little harm and a lot of good in having your wings clipped; in fact, it will save you a lot of aimless wandering, and me a lot of bother."

Growing in my heart, from that same deep region by which I withstood the calling of my name, strength rose to my mouth, and words with it, "It is you who speaks of freedom, not I. When you speak you miss my mark by a long way, for I despise your offerings. Your freedom makes man an animal whose mind is chained to the perch, and you the keeper of the zoo. I look not for that. In fact, I do not look for freedom at all. I look for myself, for who I am."

Dorran-ap-Lusdburn's superiority was devolving into shock as I spoke, "And while I am in your world…"

"My World? *My World?*" he interrupted, almost screaming. "This is ours; it befits both of us to be here."

"No!" I objected, "How can this world be mine when my heart yearns for another? While I remain here, I will never be me. The lies! The deception! The confusion! Here, certitude is impossible."

"Spare me your bathos. You are who I say you are," the old man countered. "Nothing more! Be certain of that."

"I do not know who I am, but I know I am not anything you would have me to be. I am much less than you say, and much more. I am confident of this: There is One who knows who I am; and through that door I go seeking His answer."

Resistance had achieved its necessary task. The nocuous state receded and illusion vanished. Chemosh's shoulder was still pinned to the wall, the invisible burden of defeat weighed heavily upon him. Levering my foot against his chest, I claimed victory, "I'll have my sword back now." Wrenching the blade free, I returned to the portal's door.

What transpired was truly amazing for out of the earth's bowels words rumbled throughout my limbs, and exploded from my mouth, *"Bardur Tesun... Barrashion!"*

I struck the door with Nepsis' star and my voice filled every vacant space in the universe, commanding, "Open! And let me through!"

Open it did.

Stark brightness made it impossible for me to see where my first foot would fall. I was about to step forward, when a stampede of people rushed on me from the other side. They had been crowding the door, ready to surge through the opening. I am sure they would have crushed me had I not been holding Nepsis. Despising the light, they fell left and right, tumbling, and crashing, and fighting their way into The Hankering House, filling the room with thrashing arms and tangled legs, and tumultuous shouts and rantings. Chemosh and the Candyman leaped out the door into the desert and I saw them no more.

I moved against the press, my breath held tight, I stepped into the light, but gravity withstood me. I could not make that final leap, that leap of faith. That was the moment a hand reached for me through the crowd. It was scarred, but it was strong, and it took hold of me and lifted. In that hand, I was as light as air.

Below I saw a sea of people. The world became as large as the universe and then shrank to the size of a pearl. I knew I was free.

And with that knowledge came a great Thud!

CHAPTER 17

The End of Madness

Good! "You have returned." A strong, yet sympathetic, voice hovered over me; but I could not distinguish any face. I had fallen out of bed and onto my head. The Voice was returning me to my crib and back under covers.

"Thought we had lost you: What, with your fevers, your ulcerated body, swollen tongue and throat, you could barely breathe. But you have the blood of kings in you, there is no doubting that; and it will take more than fever to summon your doom."

"I can't see." Reaching for my eyes, I felt bandages wrapped round my head, and instinctively started peeling them off.

"Not yet, Orson." My two hands were firmly restrained. "You have not used your eyes for many years, except for when I have called them open. We will remove the bandages later, as the sun approaches the sea. Tomorrow, or perhaps the next, your eyes will contest with the full light of day. For now, you need sustenance." The voice summoned another, "Suso, bring food and water. Our young prince has stirred."

Strange aromas soon confronted my nostrils as soup and bread were placed before me.

"Suso, I present to you the future of Moranor. A savage and a madman you called him; and that he was. Yet, he will teach you the foolishness of hasty words. For not every savage is thoroughly savage, nor are all madmen completely mad. Some are mad because the world's insanity prevails and casts perception and judgement into the asylum. Others are mad by choice, until, driven mad by their madness, they determine to leave madness behind. I trust your service to him these past two years has gained you grace in his eyes. If so, your life may yet fulfil its calling. Now feed him, and get him moving. I go to prepare the way. You have seven days to strengthen him for the journey ahead."

I supped while Suso talked, "Forgive me sir, I have been a fool; too hasty and judgemental. They brought you in, naked and filthy, matted hair down to your waist. You looked like a barbarian. Screaming, and groaning, and grunting were your only language; but it was I who was mad and whose words were barbaric and ignorant. For that, my lord, you could cast me aside. Mind, you'd be losing a faithful servant. I have looked after you these past two years; I, and no other! Made your bed, fed and clothed you, wiped your vomit and kept you clean. When the moon was full, it was I who saved you from inflicting damage upon yourself. So, I place my life in your hands, and hope that mercy flows through veins of royalty."

My mouth opened to reply; utterance, initially denied, eventually rasped across my throat, "Aye, mercy, and justice. I will not make the first judgement of a sane mind that of censure, and I have no notion of any wrong you may have committed. I know, however, that I am in debt to you, and I thank you for all you have done. I must have been a great burden." With those few words my breath reached its end.

"Speak no more, my lord. You need your strength. After eating we must rise and have your body moving. I've been walking you every day, well dragging you mostly. Today you begin to regain your legs, and by week's end you will need to run."

It happened as Suso said; once my stomach was full, I was out of bed. With considerable effort, I paced a room I could not see; Suso guiding my steps, his shoulder bearing much of my weight. Outside on the balcony, I could feel the cold breeze sweeping across my skin. My legs lacked substance and condition; they did all they could, until, lathered in sweat, I reclaimed my bed.

As the sun set, bandages were removed. I opened my eyes to a blur; vague images fused together, and then fell apart. Slowly, focus captured form, until I could see with a welcome degree of clarity. Suso lifted me from the bed and helped me walk, a little longer and stronger this time; even a length of the room without assistance. Alongside the balcony's pillars, delighting in my newfound sight, I feasted on the burning sky: purples, and reds, and the darkening deep of the ocean, I drank in waves that crashed against the castle wall below, I thrilled at the sea eagle diving for its final feed of the day, and I welcomed the wind in my face. I was alive!

Waking, as the morning's light leached through the bandages that protected my eyes, a beautiful woman sat at the foot of my bed, her eyes bathing me with tender affection. Her words sang of healing and strength, of life and love.

Suso entered, his voice a harsh contrast to the fair lady, who had mysteriously absented herself. Light diminished with her parting. Suso expressed surprise that I was washed and wearing new clothes. "It must have been the woman whose song woke my morning." I conjectured.

Suso remained adamant, no women have entered the castle for many a year. "Perhaps Alne has paid you a visit?" he laughed.

I did not find him funny at all (it would take quite some time for my sense of humour to develop), and was about to tell him so, when bread, soaked in soup, silenced my lips. A rigorous regimen of exercise was apportioned me, which I executed blindly until the fourth morning, whereupon my eyes were set free of their bonds, and, for the first time I could see all things with a degree of clarity.

After breaking fast, I was toured through the castle. I'd walked half the morning before my strength waned. With food and rest we ventured outside again. Early winter's chill crisped the air, and a grey sky threatened rain. Few soldiers manned the walls, fewer still walked the yard; their scarcity was notable.

"There are reasons." Suso said in reply to my thoughts. "Now let's find you a suitable mount."

A narrow alley led to a large hall stabling twenty finely tuned horses. Suso explained to the guard our requirements, receiving more respect than I expected, whilst I, being ignored, received none. We promptly left the stables, with Suso astride a formidable black stallion of at least seventeen hands, and me, sat on a fat thing, barely larger than a pony. A fast walk took us under the portcullis. "Do not think the guard rude, my lord." Suso apologised, once we were away. "Your identity is kept secret, even from the soldiers of Amaras. Uriel has warned them concerning the folly of curiosity." Fanuilos, as my horse was known, frequently broke its gait merely to keep pace with the other horse.

Except for a long, thin isthmus arching a crooked finger toward the mainland, the castle was surrounded by ocean. Waves crashed against the bony appendage and stirred up a foamy mist through which we passed. Once on the mainland, we launched into a full gallop. Leaning low beside a thick, lunging neck, we thundered over field and hill. He might not be pleasant to the eye, and no doubt other horses mocked him, but Fanuilos had an amenable, eager character and I quickly found myself appreciating his good nature. On that perfect afternoon, on that perfect horse, I was as free as the wind.

We returned just as the gates were being shut; horse and rider both in a-lather. "Good!" Suso laughed. "You will be more than ready come Uriel's return."

CHAPTER 18

The Journey to Eden

On the seventh day of my waking, I recognised the voice of him who first greeted my re-engaging with this world. "Out of bed, young lord! The new day beckons us to adventure."

I found myself staring into the face of history, "Good sir! You seem familiar. How is it I know you?"

He smiled, "You are not mistaken. In your youth I was your adviser, as I was your father's adviser before you, and his father's, before him, and so on and so forth. I am Uriel, at your service."

"Uriel? I might know that name."

"You know it, well enough. When last together, you were but a boy." Uriel launched into a brief tragedy, "Your father was killed in the Battle of Esgaroth. Whereupon, you were made king: Too soon! The throne was your ruin! Robbed of a father to inspirit your humility; surrounded by leeches baying for your blood; pride claimed the throne for its own. There followed years of unruly and unguarded debauchery in which deceit and treachery festered, culminating in a conspiracy between your cousin, Rochal, and Saba, ruler of Sabbaea. They took you captive and imprisoned you in the Citadel of Vanitas, or Vanity as I prefer to call it. Your wife and family were slain. Rochal, taking the crown by force, ordered any semblance of you be stricken from Moranor. In time you were forgotten, but your father was not. He was a righteous king, Celorn the Sublime, a god of this world. It is in his memory that the Valoria remain true, refusing allegiance to your cousin, Rochal. It was they who helped me rescue you from the hands of Saba."

"Who are the Valoria?"

"They are The Mighty, The Puissant; they are The Grey Hoods, knights of royalty; loyal to your father's throne. Except for the Sons of Eden, no force in this world compares with them. Come now," Uriel placed his hand on my shoulder, "We speak too long. I will answer all your questions on the way."

Food entered the room as Suso exchanged places with Uriel who was already out the door, his voice trailing behind, "I'll make sure everything is right for the road."

By the time I finished the necessary ablutions Uriel returned ushering us to horse. We were well on our way before dawn etched a jagged silhouette on the horizon, and the sun was well past its apex before lethargy stole my muscles. Uriel had been talking about the days of my father when he noticed my concentration waning, so we veered off-road and rested, washing down bread with refreshment savouring similar to Suso's soup. "The drink contains everything you need for your health." I grimaced at the strong flavour. Suso smiled almost apologetically, "Its ingredients come directly from Uriel's Garden. Bitterness is not the fault of the soup, for it is wholesome; it is your taste that is bitter, not the food. Soon, that which seems bad will taste sweet."

"I am glad for it. I feel stronger with every mouthful."

"Then, if you feel up to it, we'll get moving." Uriel directed, mounting his horse. "Until your body is fully recovered, I would rather not have you spending the night outside. That means we'll need to reach The Immaculate Haven before midnight."

The journey allowed me time to broach some questions: "I counted the garrison protecting the castle, and saw no more than twelve, including the stable guard. It strikes me as far too few for such a fortress."

"Strength is not measured by number alone," Uriel replied. "Sometimes the stronger we appear the more vulnerable we become. We secured your freedom from The Dark Tower and sailed immediately for Vanroma's Citadel, the fortress of Jesur ap Vanroma, Vanroma the Just. We had five days advantage before Saba could reach Avalon and inform Rochel of your escape. So, the Valoria remained with Vanroma and I took you by night to Amaras, the stronghold which these two years past has secured your healing and restoration. You sighted few guards because safety lay not in numbers but in secrecy. We needed time, and a large force would draw unwelcome attention. Better to have your enemies distracted. Best have them forget about you. Rochel's arrogance was sufficient to ensure it happened as we wished. Until recently, he believed you remained at Vanroma's Citadel; moreover, he considered your physical deliverance inconsequential as long as Chemosh possessed your soul."

Immediately my body wrenched into spasm, uncontrollably twitching and shaking. Uriel reached over, grabbed my shirt, and drew my face level with his own. The spasm abated, leaving me pierced by eyes of stern rebuke, "Never let that name move you again!"

"I assure you my reaction was unintentional."

"Your reaction, intentional or not, was the vexation of fear. The only power Chemosh has is what you grant him. If you give him your fear, he will take your soul. Fear God and Him alone! I did not carry you through the caverns of hell to have you enslaved again to that which has been conquered. You are free now. Do not let imagination drag you back to the underworld."

I sighed, "I thought it all a marish dream."

Uriel replied, his voice calm and practical, "Aye, but real if we make it so; and the reason why we must make haste now, for Rochel serves Chemosh. Were

Rochel not so proud The Ugly would have been alerted all the sooner. Pride, as always, is their undoing. Now that you have done the impossible and returned from hell's kitchen, an alarm will have reached Rochel's ear and stirred him to action. He will leave no stone unturned in his search for you."

"Good! I would that Rochel were here now: Everything within me would repay him for his treachery."

Uriel frowned, "Tell me, have you remembered your name?"

"No, well maybe; I was called me Dorranor."

"Dorranor, son of Dorran-ap-Lusdburn: *son of Chemosh*. Yes, that was a name you were given, one of many you took upon yourself; but neither that name, nor any other that you bore were the real you. In your weakness, darkness took your name, and gave you others of less worth. You have battled that darkness, all the vein and futile characters created through egotistical pursuits and the surrender of integrity. And I have battled with you. In every crisis, I attended you, willing you on. I was the raven burrowing into your prison cell, bringing you light; I sent the star, Philokalia, to guide you through the desert; I waged the battle for your soul, and did not relax my will until you leaped through The Door. That was the unmaking, the decreation. But you are still weak. You have not yet been made. The law of the universe is: *That which is empty must be filled!* Were you to face Rochel ahead of time, hatred and vanity would rush into the vacant place. Though you slay him, your soul would join his in similitude."

Uriel spoke for the duration of that day, filling even the silence between words with wonder as he explained my journey out of the caverns of the damned. I listened until the setting sun glistened upon the golden rooftops of The Immaculate Haven. My eyes surveyed the land, amazed, my gaping mouth bespeaking wonder.

"We crossed the borders of Eden several leagues back," Uriel smiled, "Did you not see the guardian? This world is much larger than from whence we came, but most never see into it, until it is too late. Many behold it from afar. Few cross the threshold; you have to have the key. It is like passing through the eye of a needle. The ignorant consider it a myth, as they do Atlantis. The fabricated legends of Atlantis are told and retold because Atlantis prefers peace, choosing isolation, remaining insulated from the rest of the world. Occasionally, men have emerged from here and there and become great kings, that was their destiny and choice. Such are the Valoria; such are nobles, heroes, and saints. The world is unworthy of them, for they are not of the world. Eden is more open than Atlantis, more receptive, but no less serious or mysterious. We have ridden into the most serious kingdom in the universe. Once entered, it enters you, and will never leave. The vision will either haunt or inspire you throughout eternity."

CHAPTER 19

The Immaculati

L iving water tumbled past the village. Colour of sky and earth, grass and tree appeared, as far as I could tell, to be original and alive; I supposed every colour in the world received its inception here. Drawing air was akin to the first breath of life. I was imbibing the verve of Eden, and felt I had been transported to rhapsody.

Ahead, two women emerged from the tree line bearing the offerings of the forest. They waded across one of the streams that passed each side of the village, and filed past me without acknowledgment, heading directly for a large building that later I discovered was The Great Hall.

Suso found me bathing in the stream. My skin was as blue as the sky. He berated me for risking the progress of my health. I took little notice; the mountain flow was alive to me. He entered the water complaining that he bathed but a week before and was not due another for at least three more. Apparently, I was highly capricious. Being a man of unusually large proportion, Suso could easily have tossed me onto dry land, but respect staid his hand. Instead, waist deep in the cold flow, he bargained for my extraction; finally succeeding when the icy chill had quieted his tongue and simultaneously set his teeth rattling. We made for our room and the warmth of an open fire.

Fully expecting to resume our journey, surprise, and some disappointment, confronted me as Suso related that Uriel dismissed himself late the previous evening and would be away for an unspecified time. Meanwhile, we were guests of Eden.

"A day or two here will serve us well." Suso offered. "It is said that there is magic in the air. Meaning, the air will do you good."

"I can believe that! In one morning, every inch of my aching body feels soothed. Nevertheless, I would prefer to be on our way. Vengeance is my desire; to meet my adversary and send him to hell."

"All in good time, my lord. For now, you must make do with more tender fare: The Lady whose guests we are."

"Eden?"

"Yes, tonight we join her table for a feast;" adding with a grin, "I can taste the food and wine already."

The day lingered, though not uneventfully, and never monotonously; the village was alive, at least that was how it felt. I put time's expanse down to a somewhat apprehensive anticipation of meeting The Lady of Eden. But another reason gradually dawned: To say "slowly," would be using the wrong word, a careless, hasty word; it would be more appropriate to suggest the day passed meaningfully; for every little thing bore its reason, and each moment was worthy of attention. With the passing of time, I delighted in finding the meaning of everything.

It became increasingly apparent that Eden was overwhelmingly the domain of women. Not that men were absent, but there weren't many present. Any want of masculine aptitude, however, was compensated through ingenuity and resolute camaraderie. There was no mistaken identity: the ladies of Eden were not trying to be men; they would not do what a man should do. They were as women ought to be; thoroughly original, fearsome in the best sense of the word, undeniably beautiful, and uncompromisingly feminine. No man could gaze at The Immaculati without finding himself arrested and enraptured; he who does not, is not a man!

A voice breached my musings, "Many of Eden's sons are engaged in the great war," the sound was captivating and compelling, arresting and enchanting. "Those born outside of Eden are disappointing, weak and unmanly; betrayed by passion and apathy, defeated, desperate, yearning for affection and attention, burning with lust and envy; unmanly, in the sense that they let their feelings, needs, and weakness master their intellect and calling." I turned, and saw standing in the doorway, with dark hair falling over lithe shoulders, one of the shield-maidens of Eden. Her head bowed deferentially; her warm, invasive eyes suspended time. This woman would win wars before they even commenced. She continued, "With the exception of the Atlanteans, no man ventures here from outside without trepidation. Many hear the call, but few are chosen. Finding the key to a world they wish they had never entered, they depart, captivated and intimidated." Her words sang with compassion, but it was not until she introduced herself that she actually moved her lips. "I am Monét. I have been asked to bring you to The Lady of Light."

Her eyes relaxed slightly, enough to loosen my tongue, "Greetings, Monét. I would tell you my name, but I have lost it. I can think of no greater pleasure than to accompany you to your Lady."

Through passage and street, we talked. I could not help but ask, "What brought you to refer to the strange absence of men?"

"I heard your mind's reflection."

Immediately I determined that while here I would mind my own business.

"You need not be concerned. It is good that I could hear your mind-talk. All thought should be so clear; like a lucid pool. Many are too confused and lack the mental strength necessary to muster clarity; they are muddy waters. Still others don't think at all; they are lazy, empty, dry; such have lost their mind."

"I lost mine. Only recently did I find it again." I spoke with sudden recollection.

"You lost your name *and* your mind?" her voice bordering between sadness, censure, and amusement, "Well, one is bound to lead to the other."

I felt her probing my memory. Perhaps she was trying to help unearth my name. However, I reminded myself to guard my thoughts.

Monét laughed; a sound, fresh as rain in summer and warm as sunshine in winter, "You may be able to keep some secrets from me, but save your strength if you think you can keep anything from She who wields the Sword of Light."

And with that we quieted, for we were walking the colonnade toward the Great Hall. Guards lined the perimeter; terrible beauty standing afore, white marble behind. Twin doors lined with gold opened to our advance and we entered a festive arena.

The hall was a hive of music, dancing and laughter, the entertaining and the entertained, archers displaying their skill, athletes competing. Everything seemed to unfold with orchestrated harmony. Monét led me on a precise path through the centre of it all. Tables were festooned with bountiful delight. We approached a group, several maidens whose laughter danced with the music. As one they separated, and she who had been the centre of attention stood, greeting, "Welcome young prince, welcome to my Garden. Too long have we awaited your return from doom."

I looked upon perfection, and was speechless. Her eyes were deep hypnotic pools, into which I fell. Water rushed past my ears whispering:

Open your eyes, open your eyes.
The dawning has begun.
Open your eyes, open your eyes;
All evil is undone.

The waters flowed over my face and I could breathe no more.

"Have you nothing to say to The Lady?" Monét had assumed a guard-like position behind Eden, and though her lips were pursed and unmoved, her intent was clear and commanding.

I gasped; air rushed into my lungs and words babbled from my lips, "My eyes threaten to erupt, for I look upon beauty transcendent, and from this moment I will be haunted by your vision."

"Impudence!" Monét struck telepathically.

"No need to protect my honour, Monét, it has not been slighted." Eden interceded, her voice a mesmeric song. "The young prince is barely beginning his life. Far too many have I seen born old and die young. Here is one who died old, yet is being born anew. We will not berate him for speaking his heart."

"Are you hungry? Thirsty? The food from this land will surely satisfy the wonderer's appetite."

"I was hungry, my Lady, but no pangs trouble me now."

"At the very least you will drink the welcoming cup with me."

A golden chalice passed from The Lady Eden's lips to my own, the sweet wine poured through me till its effect could be felt in my fingers and toes. "May your stay here prove as profitable as it is welcome."

I was given the chair alongside hers. Suso was already seated to my right; a large piece of venison in one hand, a half-drained goblet in the other, and a satisfied smile completed his face.

Eden faced the gathering. Without word or signal, all activity ceased and attention was fastened upon her. "Two guests join our meal: Anselm, son of Aneurin the Invincible and Aurelia, Daughter Immaculate. Many are the days since you last favoured us with your company."

A wave of applause swept through the hall. Suso bowed to The Lady, then looked at me and winked.

"Also, here is one whose name is being won: Son of Celorn the Sublime and Gwenlorra, Daughter Immaculate."

This evoked an ovation of awe from all; and though it seemed common practice in this place to speak one's mind without moving one's lips, some mouths did indeed open and marvel, while others spoke through wondering eyes.

Eden locked her eyes on mine, space faded into black as I found myself once again in pools of rushing water bearing words that filled my soul, "All creation has been waiting for this day. To the mountains you go to find your strength; through water to discover depth; and desert to muster endurance. Wisdom you must gain; enough to raise an army from the earth. Great danger lies before you, death snaps at your heels. When the time is fully come, and all that is necessary is formed, seek your destiny on the fields of Acheron where you shall fight for truth, liberty, justice and the honour of your name."

CHAPTER 20

The Beatific Vision

When the trance receded, I saw everyone occupied with their various entertainments. Suso was dancing, and Eden's face lit bright with laughter. I alone was aware of her prophecy.

"Eat, drink," her eyes directed, "let us celebrate your return to the free-world."

The meal was exquisite. I was feasting upon the bountiful fare when I thought, "The food here is resourceful; the earth is rich, the water and air pure and undefiled. This is how things were in the beginning. A hundred fruits from the outer-world could not contain the life of a single apple from our orchard." Monét, ever watchful, was once again invading my mind, "It is from here that all life in the world springs."

"Will you kindly cease that?" I adjured, "It is not good manners to enter someone's mind without warning. Further, if you don't mind, I am used to seeing lips move when being spoken to."

"The Lady Eden requests your presence. She waits outside."

I followed, surprised to find the sun at his apex; we had been in the hall for many hours and the daystar ought to have been well set. A hundred paces ahead, gracing the river's bank, a tall marble statue guarded her domain; a feminine deity, identical to the woman who woke me in Amaras. I heard Eden's compelling voice whispering upon the breeze, "What have you seen since arriving, young prince?" I looked for Eden, but Monét was the only person present. Again, the voice spoke, "Tell me, what can you see?"

'I'll tell you what I can't see,' I thought. 'I can't see you.'

"Look again." Suddenly, the statue was beside me reaching for my hand. Her porcelain skin was warm, tender, and full of life.

"My Lady!" I gasped. "Since being here, the most wondrous sights have filled my eyes; from the mighty mountains to the golden hall."

"So, your vision extends to the mountains? Well done! They are beyond the sight of many. It is for this reason that Uriel brought you here, so your eyes could be opened. You have escaped the dread where illusions abound. Mark my word, there is no illusion here. This is why those we welcome seldom remain; accustomed to the robes of illusion they feel naked and impoverished without them. Illusion fills man with disillusion. This is why my mother and father ran after the falling, and why The Loving Light gave me charge over Eden, commissioning me protector and keeper of the gate, placing in my hand the flaming sword, barring the false intruder." Her hand moved swiftly; dazzling light flashed; sound, felt, more than heard, reverberated through the atmosphere. She raised her hand high and in it was a sword, and lightning danced across the heavens.

"This is Illuvitar, sword of the Cherubim, Sword of Truth and Light."

I gasped. It was identical to the blade I found in the dungeons of Chemosh.

"Yes, you know Illuvitar. You have felt his might. Uriel requested the sword's presence in the quest for your salvation. Had you known the awful power in your possession the caverns of the damned would have burst asunder and a multitude come forth in your train. But you did see him, and that was no mean feat; more than that, you wielded him to the level of your knowledge. He, in turn, allowed you to handle him and served you as he could, for he serves The Loving Light."

Eden sheathed Illuvitar; the atmosphere quieted, and Eden's eye's softened, "Now, open your eyes and look at me."

Although I had been looking at her, I sharpened my focus, the intent of my will fastened upon her eyes. In doing so, as in the great hall, all sensorious affectation vanished into black and nothing remained but her.

"What do you see?"

"I do not have words to describe."

"You must try."

"I see Life! Purity! Beauty! Strength! the Sublime! Immortality!"

"You do well, but your eyes merely penetrate the surface of things. Were you able to pierce the core of creation, to peel back every layer, to see what lies beyond the elemental, to infiltrate earth, wind, and fire: What would you see then?"

"That I can answer, for the layers are repealing as you speak: It is all glorious, all wonderful, it is light and life; it is beyond my knowledge, yet it fills me with knowing; I would venture to say I see The Dawn of Creation, the Alpha and Omega, the Beginning and the End, the Life of He Who is All and in all, He who Uriel calls *The Mysterium Tremendum*."

Offering neither acknowledgement nor correction, Eden directed me to the mountains which suddenly appeared much closer than I remembered, "They are beautiful, are they not? When you survey those painted peaks, what is your response?"

"I behold them and feel humble and strong."

"You respond appropriately, and those feelings resonate and reciprocate the beauty of the mountain; a terrible beauty, a fearsome beauty, a strong, powerful majesty."

"Look now, high above them."

I turned my attention to the sky and immediately the sun began to set: Red, purple, and orange exchanged intensity, rushing across the heavens before fading into the horizon.

"Again, tell me what you see."

"I behold the thrill of eternity, the contrast of vibrant energy and vast tranquillity. Also, I sense sadness, for what is before me fades into night, to be lost forever."

"Nothing that enters you can be lost, unless you are lost. All things held within your heart are yours eternally, for good or for evil. Your sadness arises because you assume beauty has an end in itself. All things on this earth that we take for ends are in fact means. Beauty exists because it is the love of The One penetrating materiality, drawing you to Him."

Into my hand Eden placed a white dove, "Now, what comes with your reflections upon her, fairest among birds?"

"Purity, elevation, fragility."

"All your responses resonate with truth. The beauty of the dove is its very fragility, just as the lily of the field is beautiful because it is fragile. Such things live on the edge of existence, in absolute dependency upon The Loving Light."

Then, with a lilting voice, she plied, "What of my Immaculati, are they not beautiful?"

A sheepish glance at Monét almost robbed me of words, "It is well known that The Most-High has granted beauty to woman, but I have never seen any as fair as the women of Eden. They are beauty personified, and yet there is something even more appealing, something I cannot put my finger on."

"You dare not place your finger on any of us!" Monét warned, with the barest brushstroke of a smile.

Eden's amusement was more noticeable, "The women of this land possess, above all other things, order; without order, beauty degenerates into anarchic mass. Their physical presence is but the culmination of internal symmetry; they struggle not within themselves, there is no division and consequently no degradation. Their beauty endures for they are not allured by anything less than The One. Beauty is Eternity here below. All their actions are measured accordingly; a line of truth flowing from heaven to their hearts."

"Young prince," Eden continued, "you possess true vision, albeit in its formative stage. You have the seed of the seer! Keenly you discern the end from the beginning. Mountains and streams and oceans and flowers and animals and birds and man and woman are conduits through which we behold The Loving Light; every response corresponds to true Beauty, to the ideal Good, to the infinite aspects of Absolute Personality. Through your senses these visions enter your soul and become part of you. You feast upon them as surely as you consume a meal. In this way you become a partaker of The Most-High. To misperceive is death. To apprehend is Life!"

My lesson concluded; we made our way back to the village. It was noon again. I took the opportunity to comment on what seemed to be an unusually lengthy day. "Men have become prisoners of time," she sang, "Days and nights and seasons ought never to be narrow and restrictive; yet they do serve a purpose. Alternating ambience enables us to see and experience much more than we could were we captives of any particular moment. We would never understand the vast dimensions of the universe were there constant day, nor would we appreciate spring if there were no winter. There is another reason for day and night and the passage of time, it is so man might learn to number his days appropriately and not be lost in space. But here in Eden we have no need for such numbering: Time serves us according to our need."

CHAPTER 21

The Bard's Song

In the great hall, all attention was focused upon a bard announcing his song:

"The Noble Atlantean"

Eager reception indicated the song's popularity. The bard's earthy tone captured the swell of the ocean, all at once the atmosphere began ascending and descending, condensing and expanding, restraining and elating:

In the days of good and evil in the land of Moranor
The country woke one morn and change was in the air;
Boreas turned foul and on his stinking breath
A tide of evil swept o'er sea and land and bore
From the North in varying and vicious form
Griffin, wolf, serpent and storm;
But most vicious by far was the wind: it was ill!
The land fell to sickness; man, beast and plant withering.
Until a cry of great despair forced the gathering
Of Moranor's High Council.

PARALLEL WORLDS

Together in Avalon's Hall they joined mind and heart.
Erastas King and Thera his Queen,
The Seven warriors of The Mark:
Boros, Andur, Tassun, Boz, Jarrad, Platin, and Venarr,
Dwaiin and Sophian priests, and wisest by far.
But when no answer was forthcoming
It was given unto The Seven
To seek and find solution from The Old Man of The Sea

O'er oceans nary travelled,
On Tassun's golden ship they sailed
Till The Old Man was discovered
Walking Oceania's waves
"You seek to know why the ill wind blows."
The Old Man crowed as the billows rolled
"It blows because of negligence.
For innocence is found in the dragon's lair,
Verona, Erastas' virgin daughter,
Is bound in torment there.
Captive prisoner of evil most foul,
The Chimaera has her locked in the forgotten tower.
Now let all who hear me rest assured,
Boreas will heal once her freedom's secured.
For Verona, fair flower of Moranor,
Alone sweetens the air."

The Seven paled and gasped
While The Old Man cautioned, "Beware!
Courage and veracity alone can enter Nemesis' lair
Any wearing poorer armour

Upon death do venture there."
The Seven returned to Moranor and told the Council all
Erastas' kingly pride demanded,
"It is for The Seven to heed the call."

"I will go!" said Boros.
And all agreed he should;
He was bravest of the Seven,
And his heart was mainly good.
A full day's ride he journeyed
To mountains long forgotten
With all his heart intending
Iin the morn to slay the dragon.
But the Chimaera, with evil cunning,
Determined Boros would miss the dawning,
And came in feminine form
Clothed in nothing but the mist.
Boros' weakness therein was lit.
And taking his eyes she left him blind,
Aimlessly wandering the mountainside,
Where blindly falling he did quit.

Andur arose with strength of heart
Assuring chastity he would guard.
He rode the day and hunger burning,
Declined fighting dragons
Until his stomach stopped yearning.
His belly stirred by aromas wafting,
Luring him in to The Forgotten Inn.
Entering, he beheld a kingly feast,

The strength he'd need to slay the beast.
Gladly handing his money over,
Eating till haply 'til he did slumber:
A sleep from which he would never recover.
Too much the glutton, he vomited.
By morning Andur was also dead.

The honour fell next to Tassun,
Who being of the ocean
Navigated an alternate course,
Anchoring his vessel at Metaxu's source.
Thrilled with adventure and indifferent to danger,
He scaled the Forgotten Throne,
And entering the dragon's lair
Believed himself alone,
For Verona and the dragon were not home.

But he did espy treasure, and
Fancying some for personal pleasure,
Filled his arms with many a charm.
His ears then pricked to a muffled cry,
Beyond the fortune there he spied,
Strongly bound and firmly tied
Erastas' beautiful daughter.
Quickly he ran to lend his hand,
But the ground o'er which he spanned
To his demise was sinking sand.
And the weight of all his plunder
Dragged the voyager down and under.

THE BARD'S SONG

Erastas, dismayed when golden sails
Returned not to the harbour,
Called the four remaining knights
To join him in the chamber.
Commanding them to quest together
Pleading, nay demanding,
They go redeem his daughter.

Arriving at Nemesis' lair,
Venarr adjured, "This is not fair!
There is no honour in facing a beast together,
I will go alone. And you? Be at your leisure."

But Platin's rivalry increasing
Fuelled envy, not tolerating
Kudos awarded to one so undeserving.
Accustomed to their green debate,
Boz laughed and closed his weary gaze,
Till eventual decision they did make.

Jarrad, impetuous, and full of rage,
Refused to sit and negotiate,
Rushed in and on to the dragon's stage.
Two eyes of evil spied he leering,
So thrashing and lashing with spear and sword,
Till eventually his strength exhausting,
The dragon made of him quick sport;
Like cat with mouse, before quietly consuming.

PARALLEL WORLDS

Sweet Verona saw the devouring,
Her piercing screams the others alerting,
Who, ceasing arguing, ran into the lair.
Neither Jarrad nor dragon lingered there,
They had alighted and taken to air,
From where Nemesis fell on Boz.
Robbed through apathy of the time
Necessary to clear his sleepy eyes
Before the flames surrounded.
And crisply he did die.

And then there were two, both who knew
Together they could overwhelm a dragon.
But standing not together
Fashioned their dilemma,
Ensuring they did die alone
Both slain by the Chimaera
When she came upon her throne.
Unleashing fury's scorn upon them,
In a swarming plague she flew first at Platin.
Vennar saw her but held his tongue,
'Till Platin lay wasted on the cavernous ground.

Instant remorse stole Vennar's wit;
Presumption made him the easy target.
And he fell in shame behind a watery mask;
Betrayal's tears stream o'er vanity's task.
The warriors' quest, intention grande,
But The Seven never stood a solitary chance;

THE BARD'S SONG

None possessed the noble tone
That's soft as a flower and strong as stone.

Upon the breeze news unkind
Did reach Erastas and stole his mind.
So, Thera commanded Dwaiin and Sophian
To bring an end to the evil wind.
And they made a call throughout the land
"Men of integrity and courage arise,
Deliver Verona from Chimaera's devise."
But the call spread terror in every heart
Virtue wasn't near; Neither was it far
For it so happened Atlanta had sent a son to Eden,
Who, passing quietly through the land,
Was moved by Moranor's predicament.
And heeding the priestly call
Journeyed to the dragon's den.
Determined not to fall,
Being virtuous and vigilant,
He lingered not along the way,
But swiftly scaled the steep ascent,
Chimaera's eye astray.
And finding Nemesis asleep
Upon the serpent's treasured heap,
Secretly, he stole fair Verona away.

Upon the waking
Chimaera's wrath was raging;
She loathed the cheating of her prize.

She lept on her dragenous pet, ascending,
Determined to bring the Atlantean's demise.
Down the Forgotten Mount they flew,
Down upon the fleeing two.

But the Atlantean wielded a secret shield,
Armour invisible, stronger than steel;
Nothing in him could the dragon sear,
His heart stood master over fear
Vengeful, the Chimaera morphed
Into the plague. She turned upon the flower.
In harms way the Atlantean walked,
Shielding the beautiful Verona.
And bearing Chimaera's swarming curse,
Cast himself into the dragon's breath.
The consuming fire did burn and burn,
But it was Chimaera who in flames did burst.
In terror, the dragon reared and roared.
The Atlantean reached for him and fought.
His bare hand plunged into its heart;
The dragon, sighing, breathed his last
But from the blackened pulse
Emerged a winged unicorn:
Ungründ the Magnificent.
Who bore Verona to Avalon.

His daughter returned, Erastas' mind regained,
And Moranor's flower refreshed the breeze again.
Erastas' joy erupted, "Where is the man?

> *Bring me this Atlantean."*
> *But the noble man continued to a different land,*
> *Far away in Eden.*
> *"Then tell me his name that we might send for him?"*
> *None knew, however, not even Verona.*
> *"Then I declare to him power and honour.*
> *And I grant that for all time*
> *He shall be known as Celorn the Sublime."*

"My father!" I whispered amazed.

The spellbinding atmosphere lifted; applause erupted, and the bard slowly swivelled in our direction.

"Uriel." Eden enthused taking his hands, "You enrich us with every appearing."

"I arrived just in time. Suso was about to sing, and we would never have heard the end of it." He winked at Suso who joined us, smiling, and then added, "Forgive me for bringing the abbreviated version, these are hasty times."

Of course, the length of the story was immaterial; from the moment the song began we were transported to the world of dreams and spirit; the song's words transposing into images before, and around, and within us.

"Great evil is afoot outside of your realm, my Lady." Uriel warned. "If you consider the young prince has found his sight we will be leaving."

Unexpectedly, notions of departure found me disappointed.

"His eyes are open; he has the seer's vision." Eden replied. "I know the tide of evil is rising. Since winter's end the flaming sword has been busy resisting the growing darkness on our borders."

"Winter's end?" I blurted. "But winter is only beginning."

"I have been away three months since you arrived here," Uriel answered "though it seems but a day to you. And when we depart this fair land, you will think your time here less than a moment."

"Monét." Eden directed, "Make sure the horses are ready for our guest's departure."

Within the hour the lights of Eden were a dim glow behind us. Suddenly, a flash of white light, thin and sharp surged from ground to sky, illuminating The Lady, Illuvitar's flame in hand, and Monét beside her. And if I was not mistaken, Monét's eyes were upon Suso. We swept through a wall of fire that did not burn, and then that magical land was gone; a passing dream: though often I returned there in my mind, believing the whole world would one day be restored to that faultless state.

CHAPTER 22

The Road to Fair Havens

Perhaps the transition from Eden affected my judgement, but the territory through which we rode appeared unimpressive, dull and tedious; the clear sky lacked spring's purpose, it was lifeless, drained, sapped vigourless. The life of light diminishing, in turn made the ambience engulfing. I shuddered involuntarily. Suso observed my countenance, "It always feels so to leave Eden. Everything there is much more alive than anything outside."

"True," Uriel added, "but the world has grown darker over winter, and spring has no power to alter it. It is the darkness that troubles you, young prince. Chemosh has been stirred from slumber, fear drives him to action. And Rochel has been a busy bee, calling in favours from all under the dominion of the enemy."

"What exactly is Chemosh hoping to achieve?" I enquired.

"Control! He would have this world under his rule. Impossible! He can't even control himself. Even so, he extends his influence in whatever ways he can: chaos, disorder, anarchy, rebellion; his nature presses everywhere. Yet pockets of resistance, the smattering of the noble and the innocent, exist to rub salt into his wound. Such is Eden. Because of you, my friend, The Ugly's interest in that fair land has been reawakened. From there, the archetypes of humanity exercised dominion over the entire creation. While in its infancy, Chemosh attempted to penetrate Eden and assume ascendancy over the world, of which Eden was the living womb. He succeeded and failed in one foul blow. Through deceit The Ugly secured the archetypes' allegiance, but in so doing infected all he acquired. He captured the world but it was a fallen world, a corrupt world, a lesser world, a disappointing world. But Eden he could not acquire, for in her midst grew The Incorruptible Tree, the Tree of Life, impervious, imperishable - the very opposite of his nature. Eden's existence is a constant reminder of what he does not have."

"What happened to the archetypes?"

"With their corruption, darkness infiltrated the heart of mankind and to this day manifests itself in fear; fear of everything pure and true, loving and perfect, fear of Light and Life. Eden loomed too large and terrible for them; the fallen shrank from her, ran and lived in exile. Eden's parents were the runners. Those like Eden, born before the great deception, remained true, fearsome examples of what humanity should be; they are The Immaculati. The Lady Eden was chosen guardian, Eden's vanguard, keeper of Illuvitar, The Flaming Sword. She is protector, defending all that is perfect from illegitimate access, from The Stain, from Chemosh."

It was a story to be pondered; which I did for many miles before another question sprang, "How was it that *I* drew Chemosh's attention toward Eden?"

"Well Orson, there's your lineage for a start: your mother was one of the Daughters Immaculate; your father, as you now know, an Atlantean. The purity of your heritage made you The Ugly's prize possession; seldom do the sons of the free world fall; never has any of the fallen risen again. Your emancipation has spread confusion and terror throughout the underworld. Secondly, your time in Eden was necessary, but your presence there dangerous. Not only have you breeched the gates of hell, you passed through the wall between this world and

The Beyond. When you disappeared from Chemosh's sight, The Ugly would guess you entered Eden, for Atlantis is under the waters and rarely welcomes outsiders."

I pondered why The Ugly would have to guess.

Uriel read my question, "Neither Chemosh nor his underlings can see Eden, its light is beyond them. True Light is darkness to the lost; they cannot see it. However, what they can't see tells them more than what they can. There is one final reason why Chemosh has Eden in his sights, *The Prophecy*. According to *The Book of Adam* your liberation heralds the destruction of The Ugly's kingdom." Uriel broke into a low earthy chant:

When the king returns from doom
Deliverance will he bring
He shatters the ancient tomb
The wakers rise and sing

"Words have never meant enough to Chemosh; a means to an end; a way to get his way, that's all; convenient carriers of his barrenness; a weapon to weave deceit. He understands the power, never the intent. Now he rues underestimating *The Prophecy*. Rather than parading your demise he wishes to have finished you off. Your escape served as a spur in his side. Searching the ancient books, there he read:

In the days when darkness spawns
Every terror, evil and cunning
When this world's curtain is finally drawn
And creation is come to end her mourning

The dark hand will burn on Eden's lamp
Suffering ends in the silent sound
The forgotten army revisits the land
And the fallen king, unfallen is crowned

"Prior to your liberation Chemosh considered Eden an inconvenience, but not dangerous; a prize slipped through his hand, not a flame to burn it; a carrot on the end of a stick too long, not a rod that would whip him. Now, realisation that The Good is also imminently menacing has dawned upon his dim mind and in fearful frenzy he will strike. Well, let him strike! I say, anger will blind him to our doings."

Suso, who had been riding several paces ahead, stopped and waited for us to draw alongside. He directed our attention to a cloud of dust rising in the distance, "A large force is moving slowly along the road, at least a hundred, maybe more."

"That leaves us a difficult choice," Uriel responded. "We must reach Fair Havens by nightfall, and for that we need the road, but the road means a fight. Forest and field might serve us better."

"I would rather stick to the road," Suso offered, "and enjoy the fight."

"That you would." Uriel acknowledged. "Were it you and I alone we could, but I would not risk the young prince's capture. We will leave the road."

"Not just yet," I warned. "There are scouts about; two on the hill to the right, one on the left, and five on the road's edge a league ahead."

Uriel looked, "Sabbaeans!" he spat. "How dare they pollute this fair island with their foul stench."

Out from the trees, barely a stone's throw ahead, burst horse and rider heading towards the five. I spurred my horse after him, but Uriel grabbed the reigns. "Hold. You will not catch him before he reaches his goal. Suso, take care of these few nearby. We'll deal with those ahead."

With that, Suso dismounted and disappeared swiftly into the trees on our left, returning as quickly as he'd left with blood on the end of his sword. He mounted his horse and took to the hills.

The five became six and then five again as one rider peeled toward the cloud of dust in the distance.

"Come, young prince, let us fall on them like an avalanche." Uriel then commanded the horses, "Danté! Fanuilos! Ride like the wind!"

That, we did; maybe faster. Our horses, so enthused with the chase, were magically enhanced, or so it felt to me. Fanuilos' grazing on the green grass of Eden had fared him well; no longer the laughing stock among his brethren, his coat glistened over a lean frame, and, he was taller. Though we were outnumbered, fear flew before us, turning the five on their tails. Two horses threw their riders and the rest scattered. "Suso will take care of them." Uriel declared, "We must intercept that scout."

We ran him down before he knew he was being chased. Uriel spoke a word to the raider's horse which brought him and his mount to a jolting halt. No matter how hard the rider kicked, that horse would not move.

"One more stab of your heel into his flank," Uriel admonished, "and I will let the horse kick you. Now tell me about the detachment ahead, what is its nature?"

The scout answered in a language I did not understand. Uriel pressed him with the same question from several angles.

During the brief interrogation, Suso arrived, "One of the others talked, his tongue wagged like a flag in a blustery wind. He said exactly the same thing."

Apparently, the approaching company was not an armed force but refugees fleeing the Sabbaean invaders. We also learned Rochel had promised Sabba the island if he could deliver alive the fallen prince. Of course, Vanroma and the Valoria would have to be overthrown, for they were the island's protectorate. Sabba's armada, one hundred ships complete with warriors, were besieging Vanroma's citadel as we rode. Recently Sabba learned that the fallen prince was not under Vanroma's safeguard. So, with the bulk of his army remaining at the press, scouts were dispatched, scouring the island looking for me. Sheer mischief meant they could not refrain from pillaging the towns and villages along the way.

We left the barbarian gagged and tied on the side of the road, to be swallowed up by the approaching mass.

It was as Sabba's servant confessed: a stream of refugees filed past, desolate and bleak, as only the disenfranchised can be. With nothing to offer them, except the scout's horse, some encouragement that none of the invading evil was at our back, and the assurance that we would clear the road of any at theirs, we resumed our journey to the coast.

Uriel spoke as we rode, "Sabba will be at the siege; he does not let his army venture far without him. He fancies himself something of a military strategist, just because he won a few battles against the Easterlings. He is a fool. The Valoria could dispense with him at will. It is time we need, and they purchase it for us; some, with their blood. Rochel trusts that weight of numbers will gain the citadel, and the island, and he cares little how many Sabbaeans die in the process. Yet, he puts no confidence in Sabba capturing you. As far as he is concerned you have sought sanctuary in Eden. He and Chemosh are determined to break in, bending all their will against The Sword. The Nephilim are abroad, of them we must beware. And there are other products of Rochel's evil for which we must prepare: the deforming of man and beast, and the reforming of the dragon. Rochel has also applied his mind to all things spiritual; he has read the Ancient Book, and is aware that the resurrected king ushers in The End of darkness. Before you escaped from Chemosh's dungeon he had no idea the *'king unfallen'* is you. Now he prepares Moranor for combat. Why? (He discerned my question) Because *The Prophecy* declares "*the risen king will war against the usurper.*"

I adjured, "What army will oppose him since the free-world is no longer free?"

"It is for you to raise an army and win back freedom for this world."

I was left to process my thoughts as we rode on. Uriel, determined to reach our destination before sunset, set such a pace that conversation was restricted. There was no doubting that outside of Eden, time had its limitations, and it took some adjustment on my part to come to terms with it. Everything happened slowly, or quickly, feeling either sluggish or hasty; time had not the balance that it possessed in that perfect kingdom; to one degree or another, we always seem at its mercy.

Occasional encounters with refugees, and sporadic skirmishes with Sabbean invaders, threatened to hinder, but did not prevent, our advance. Our road turned west; the countryside gradually developing the form and structure of industry, fields of barley, grazing aurochs, the emergence of fences and houses; until finally the lazy harbour of Fair Havens was in sight.

CHAPTER 23

Encounters with Atlantis

Under cover of darkness, we boarded the *Andromeda*, and set sail before first light. Evanor's silhouette rapidly retreated, reduced, and eventually rescinded behind ocean waves.

Since Eden's eye-opening lesson, my sight grew increasingly keen; so long as I did not allow mood or atmosphere to cloud the mind, my vision was penetrative. In the black of night, black against black against black, I saw; the dark form of land receding into the pitch of night, and then there was another darkness, a dangerous darkness that could be felt.

The *Andromeda* was impervious to it all; a pale golden glow emanated from her; she travelled by her own light, needing neither sun, nor moon, nor star for guidance. Her golden sails bellowed in the stiff sou-wester, and the regular rhythmical sound of bow meeting trough became strangely comforting.

Each member of the crew bore the stature of a commander; they were markedly industrious and efficient, wearing dignity bearing ardent. From below, Captain Lorenz emerged, in earnest dialogue with Uriel. They walked the deck, the captain occasionally conversing with one of his crew, instructing, where necessary. Attention was paid to every detail. Suso, he greeted warmly, as a friend well met, and me, as though related. (Some time later I discovered this was fact.) Momentarily, he stood tall and faced the wind, until satisfaction lined his face. Then he and Uriel re-immersed themselves in the hold of the ship.

"These are Atlanteans, masters over the waters," Suso enlightened, as he handed me a bowl of food, "and the *Andromeda* is an Atlantean ship. That is why she sails so luminous. It is not often that Atlanteans show themselves among the fallen. These are strange days indeed."

"*Strange* is not the word I would use. No, I would say they are a wonder, and I am grateful for every moment. The food is good Suso; you have excelled yourself."

"I am no cook, as you have already discovered. You'd be eating the grace of Atlanta, and drinking their elixir; expect your strength to be up. You'll need it; we have three days before we reach land, and I am about to teach you how to fight. Fortunately, you have a good teacher, and I, a good student. I have observed you with Uriel and The Lady Eden, you are like a sponge."

With a slap on my back, an intense course in the art of war began. Quickly it was established that I had been trained in all the basics of hand-to-hand combat; from wrestling to weaponry, single and double handed swords, mace and axe, javelin, and more, I gave an apt account. Apparent also was a distinct lack of form and fitness, "Your eye is like the eagle," Suso observed, "but your hands and feet lag; you are imbalanced and that makes you vulnerable; your muscles are soft and your mind too rigid; you need a flexible mind and a body of steel."

Suso worked me from first light to dusk. During rough weather I would climb the mast and stand on the mainsail to develop a confident bearing in the uncertain rhythm of a difficult sea. There was an exercise applicable to stretching each and every muscle to its limit. I sparred with the Atlanteans, fast with feet and hand. Suso providing constant admonishment from the side, "Let go, young prince!" He would bellow. "You are too tight, too predictable, too rigid. Let go!" I did not quite know what to "let go" of.

The constant tendency is to complicate things, to complicate the simplest of things, like life, and love, and battle. Simplicity is the secret, complication the enemy. Prediction, assumption, introspection, conjecture, projection, speculation, guessing and second guessing, it all gets in the way, creating tension, anxiety, and consequently narrowness and rigidity. Every action has an appropriate reaction; do not predict, do not be predictable, do not waste energy unnecessarily; simply do what must be done. Be swift, accurate, a sure-fired arrow streaking for the eye of the bull. Let go! Forget yourself; forget about whether you live or die, whether you are offended or injured; forget about the size of your opponent. Let go, so you might be the hand of The Most-High in the world.

Once again Suso's personality proved an engaging revelation. We were in the middle of our third afternoon on board the *Andromeda* when, between lunges, blows, and parries, he began to wax lucid, "Today I share with you the secrets of the universe: The Most-High works in and through all things. Everything He does is perfect, every movement a work of art. When united with Him we join in His song; our deeds are orchestrated at His bequest; our actions part of His Act. I hear his song in all things. When the music stops, I am out of sync." Our swords rang again and again. "There is a perfect act for every moment of your life; a time to rise and a time to rest; a time to laugh and a time to cry; a time to love. It is the same in war: Facing your enemy, there comes a time to engage and a time to withdraw; the wise heart knows the times and the procedure. There is a time to thrust and a time to parry. There is a corridor of perfection to walk on the field of battle; a path of honour; a path of life; a perfect strike path for the delivery of every weapon, a perfect posture for the body. While I walk this path, I am invincible!" Against all expectation, my foot connected with Suso's cheek, bringing a quick smile to his face. "When you hear the song on the battlefield," he continued, stopping momentarily to spit blood onto the deck, "and nothing but the song, you are more than a man, for you are in perfect synchronicity with

The Most-High. You are one with The One. It is then that the battle frenzy is come and the battle already won." And there the session concluded.

That was the first time I had ever landed a blow of any sort upon Suso; it extracted a cheer from the crew who attended our sessions with profound enthusiasm; but then, they attended everything with that same attitude. Uriel watched from the helm. Captain Lorenz called for a drink to be poured on my behalf, and with some laughter voiced, "Well done young prince. I have seen Suso take several blows by design, but to my knowledge that is the first he has ever received unintentionally."

"It was a lucky blow." I declared.

"Not lucky for me." Suso laughed. "Of a truth, in just a few days you have gained all the skills I possess, and indeed you have just bested me." His approval was generous, "You have my sword, my service and my friendship. I am yours, lord, for as long as you have need of me."

The watchman raised the alert, Moranor could be seen in the distance. With that announcement, the captain checked our speed, as he did not wish to venture close to shore before dark. With the same announcement, I drifted into myself, pondering words of prophecy and an uncertain future.

Spying me sitting on the mainsail, Uriel climbed to my side, cloak and hair tossing in the wind. "It does no good to concern yourself with tomorrow," he admonished, gazing into the distance as though piercing the mysteries of creation. "When you withdraw into yourself, your ability to see and resist darkness is diminished. In fact, when you become introverted, darkness is attracted to you; for the shadow of the soul is an abyss drawing all things into itself."

"All I have been told, the past, the prophecies, the expectations, these things loom too large," I responded. "I feel daunted, like a grain of sand before the ocean waves."

Uriel continued, "No-one, knowing the things of tomorrow feels adequate today; tomorrow won't change, but you will. In so doing tomorrow becomes what you make of it. A child can never do a man's work, but when he grows into a man he works easily. Neither can a man eat tomorrow's food today. You will find when the time is right you will be right for the time."

"Perhaps! Yet, tomorrow rushes in. I feel the future breaking upon me."

"Do not worry, the occasion approaches when time will be in your hands. The events of today and tomorrow have long been set; you simply have to play your part. For now, young prince, know that you are still in the making. Tomorrow's task, though not yet at hand, casts its shadow over you because you are not all you could be; indeed, you walk with a stoop. Were you to raise yourself to your full stature you would be taller than Suso."

That was a revelation indeed. Taller than Suso? That I had to see!

Uriel read my thoughts, "You won't *see* anything of the sort, but happen it will. Now pay attention: After we reach shore, make your way to the Forgotten Mountains. There you will find Ruâch, Master of the Sword. Beware! The dragon flies again; he has a new master: Through evil craft Rochel broke Ungründ's wings, cut off his horn, and remade the beast."

Light was fading quickly with the descending sun. Steering north we circumnavigated the peninsula, Lull to our left, Moranor to our right. I looked up at Uriel, "Will you not be going with us?"

"I am with you, but were my presence to go, your making would be incomplete. Look for me when you reach the Fields of Death. For now, I sail west with the *Andromeda*, to walk the deep where a whisper affects the whole world."

CHAPTER 24

Death Lies Near in the Wilderland

Lorenz and Uriel accompanied us ashore. We exchanged brief farewells in the shallows of a nameless bay: Uriel's final warning was that under no circumstance should we disclose my identity. A relatively easy task, for I knew not who I was. However, deep within, substance was evolving. I was becoming aware that I was no longer a nothing, nor was I the nobody who thought he was somebody and thereby descended into hell. I felt substantial; I had reason, to live! And to die. Further, the very core of my reason lay not within myself, not in my activity, nor even in my destiny, but in the knowledge that I am known by my Maker. His substantiation of my life grants me substance. I may not know who I am, but He does, and that is enough -for now.

Suso and I waded onto a gravely shore, and from there worked our way to the cliff top. Dejection's gaunt hand vexed me somewhat as I watched the translucent glow of the *Andromeda* fade into a veil beyond the sea. As she disappeared, another ship came into view, and melancholia with it. Suso saw, and broke into my silence, "You worked hard today and must be tired; we could rest a while before trekking north."

"I think we're being followed Suso. With the *Andromeda's* parting, a black sail with a red serpent appeared."

"Nephilim!" Suso cursed. "If that is the case, we should put some distance between us while we can. They are swift, but they prefer night over daylight."

We ran long and hard; we ran until despondency was displaced by determination; we ran until day dispelled night, until shadows from the Western Rise were clear and distinct upon the plane. It was in the clefts of that rocky escarpment that we sought rest. Sleep came upon me like a long-lost friend.

Hammers were pounding: the piercing sound of metal striking metal. An ocean of molten fire stretched toward the horizon, and from it a wave swelled and reached toward the sky. It gathered speed, a wall of fire and flame tumbling over me. My skin ignited, flames erupted from my eyes, mouth, ears, and heart. Yet I was not destroyed. The pounding hammers continued reverberating throughout the universe. Another fiery wave loomed; I was being shaken, overwhelmed.

A friend's hand hoisted me out of the flaming swell. My eyes settled upon Suso's familiar face, "You were having a bad dream, m'lord."

"Whether bad or good, I do not know. It looked bad, but felt good. I dreamt of fire washing over me like an ocean breaker."

Suso handed me some bread and water, "Here, eat this! The captain gave us a good supply before we left the ship." Then he offered, "It was probably the sun."

"Implying?"

"Your dream of the fire. Perhaps it was caused by the heat from the sun. It's hot enough to roast a bird in flight."

Unlike Evanor, the climate here was uncomfortable, imposing; we could feel its wasting aridity.

"I think not, I have dreamed this before. Many times, in fact. I meant to ask Uriel about it but our time together was all too brief."

"Some things are better left unexplained, especially dreams. They make themselves understood, if you know what I mean."

"No, Suso, I don't know what you mean."

"Well, if there is any more to them besides the simple ranting of the mind trying to sort itself out, then it comes to you. And, when it does you know this is that and what's what."

I sat silent, staring into the distance. I knew not the way to the Forgotten Mountains, nor, once there, how to locate Ruâch. Suso intercepted, "It will take us over five weeks if we can't get horses, three if we can; and that's just to get us to the Rumbling Ranges." Having spent much of his youth in Avalon, Suso possessed limited knowledge of the West. "Beyond them we will come upon The Rift, from which rise the Forgotten Mountains."

We shouldered provisions and descended into the Wilderland, the vast provocative terrain spanning the distance between us and the beyond. It was a desert, dry and empty, introverted and rejected. An ill wind was blowing: Upon it could be heard the sounds of sadness, and it carried the fetid odour of decomposition; a marsh, or bog, or something worse.

According to Uriel, twenty leagues north of our landing a settlement would provide shelter, information, perhaps some horses, and with any luck, a guide. Though the village was within Moranor, its distance from Avalon gave us hope that it had not fallen under Rochel's control. We had no other choice; this was the only outpost in the far west, and there was no other habitation between us and the mountains. Should we not procure a suitable guide here we would continue with blind hope.

Our road, a barely discernible track, ran three hundred paces out from the escarpment. Evidentially it had borne little traffic in recent times. The lack of footprint, either man or beast, relieved us of the notion that someone might have anticipated our arrival.

Throughout that day the rotting wind blew in our face, the smell intensifying with each step, until we were forced to mask our noses. In spite of the offensive air, we made good progress, arriving at the outpost in twilight.

The settlement emerged from the wasteland; it was uninviting and unsettling. I didn't like it. I saw no light in it.

Suso whispered, "This is Argenon. Here resides death's odorous source."

Twenty or more huts of mud and wood were arranged in a rough circular fashion, smaller dwellings on the periphery, larger and more ornate toward the centre where the community's overseer resided. We walked watchfully from one dwelling to another. There was the occasional scattering of rats and other scavengers of the night, but no human movement could be detected. On the outskirts of the town a fight broke out amongst several dogs, drawing our attention to the prize of their contention. They were fighting over entrails, human entrails that were trailing from a mound of corpses; each varying in their state of composure, but all presumably dead.

"It's the plague!" Suso rasped.

"Looks that way." I affirmed. "We'll find neither shelter nor guide in this forsaken habitat."

Leaving the dogs to their spoils we aimed to put distance between us and Argenon. The moon's cold smile provided sufficient light for a fast pace. We did not stop until Suso tugged my sleeve, "We're being followed."

"Are you certain?"

"Not long after leaving the outpost I sensed we had company. I wasn't sure at first, but someone is gaining on us. Their feet pace faster than ours."

I turned and looked behind; a fire back at the settlement lit the night sky. "What do you think we should do?"

My eyes were fixed upon the brightening glow, but Suso was more concerned about dealing with our shadow.

"We could outrun him," he suggested. "Impossible, if it is one of the Nephilim. We can catch him; you run ahead while I wait in hiding; then, I make a surprise grab. Or, we simply confront him and give him opportunity to explain himself."

"I am for the last option."

So, I called into the silence of night for the pursuant to make himself known. From the shadows, barely fifty paces behind, a figure emerged and moved cautiously toward us. Our swords glistened in the moonlight, and he stopped, "You'll have no need for those, I am unarmed." The voice was feminine; he was a she.

According to Tarryn, our shadow, seven days prior two malevolent beings, the nature of which, man or beast, was too difficult to determine, arrived at Argenon asking questions about visitors to Moranor. The villagers' ignorance enraged the antagonists, who chased down every man, woman, and child. Through fortune or guile Tarryn escaped the massacre, and hid until the callous killers departed. Possessing too little strength to dig graves for the fallen, she spent the last five days contending with dogs, pigs and more dangerous animals, gathering the departed remains and piling them into a mass pyre so as to send them into eternity with some dignity. Fear and ignorance at sight of us brought about her hiding, but closer examination convinced her we were not of the same ilk as those fiends of the genocide. There was nothing else for Tarryn to do; in desperation she finished her duty, offered a brief prayer, lit the pyre, and followed us in hope that we would provide her safe passage to the next village.

"Sadly, Tarryn," I informed, "if there can be a dissimilation of danger in these perilous times, we are taking the more dangerous route. We will not be passing near any village, and where we venture is no place for a girl."

Astute, but emotionally and physically exhausted, Tarryn collapsed sobbing; then, hastily wiped the tears and offered her services, "I have spent all my twenty-eight years in the Wilderland, and from ocean to the Forgotten Mountains,

I know the West better than most. You are strangers here, and, if I am not mistaken, in need of a guide. I will guide you, no need to pay me, simply protect me. Then, when you have finished your course, escort me to a more hospitable location." She paused, sniffed, wiped her eyes, and, hands on hips, wagered: "Agreed?"

I looked at Tarryn, tall and svelte, her face disarmingly pleasant, her demeanour, pleading yet indomitable; though her presence would prove risky, my heart could not find enough dispassion to leave her behind, "You can be our guide for as long as you keep pace with us; but I cannot ensure your safety; your life will be in constant jeopardy. You should also be warned that we will trust you for as long as you prove trustworthy; break that trust and your life will be forfeit." I offered her this, though I saw a black arrow had pierced her heart.

CHAPTER 25

Enter the Shades of the Night

The road we travelled was convenient but never secure and we no longer considered it safe. Tarryn's story confirmed we should find an alternate route. Her value as a guide was quickly substantiated, confidently leading us some twelve leagues east to where a desert stream flowed from the boggy marshes of Te Ngawha, The Boiling Springs, where the air felt much cooler. The source of Te Ngawha was the Rumbling Ranges, treacherous mountains that groan under the weight of their own gloom; rarely do any who scale those slopes return. The Wilderland blends into the Marshlands, and the Marshlands receive water from "the melts" where night ice dissolves on the Ranges' southern escarpment. This flow mixes with warm water that rises from deep underground; at all times it boils and bubbles, and its slightly acrid steam creates a permanent miasma spanning several leagues south. Many streams branch from the springs before petering into insignificance; collectively the rivulets are called Te Waeteromarama, The Waters of the Moon.

Throughout our journey Tarryn was pleasant enough, yet she remained aloof. I assumed her remote demeanour, and the growing shadow over her heart, to be caused by recent trauma. Sorrow is like an arrow in the heart of a deer; the more vigorously she tries to run, the more firmly the arrow is embedded. I did not suspect a more sinister motive.

We had been following a stream and resting in the shelter of its bank whenever our bodies demanded relief. It was on one of these occasions that Suso and I woke and discovered Tarryn's absence. The colour that flushed her face upon return betrayed duplicity. Our inquiries brought a furtive, "I was restless and scouted ahead." Her defensiveness was acute and her heart unassailably distant. The shadow had grown.

I spoke into that heart: "I have been where you are heading. Believe me when I say you do not want to venture there. The cavern of the damned is an appalling horror and there is no escape. You can be free if you resist now and turn from deception in word and deed."

A faint ray of light illuminated Tarryn's face as hope and grace was imparted; but, like storm clouds consuming a glorious sun, darkness returned: The wound was deep, "I am not prone to deception!" she pouted, "And know not to what you are referring."

"The lie is everywhere." I continued, "It wants us to believe; often appearing in the form of some good so that we reject the True Good. Swallow the lie and it will feast upon you. Already Nehushtan twists and coils, constricting and robbing you of breath; already her poison tracks through your veins and flushes your face with fear and fury."

"You think you know me!" Tarryn retorted, "When in fact it is I who know you, fallen prince. For what have you returned to Moranor? Is it not enough that we have had to endure Rochal? Do you also wish to cast *your* shadow upon the land?"

As neither Suso nor I had mentioned my identity, her snap proved the enemy was closer than we desired. I probed Tarryn further, "Deep within every human being lies the dread of being alone in the world, the dread of being forgotten by The Most-High, overlooked among the tremendous multitude. It is this fear that causes us to hate and lie and be less than we are called to be. It is this fear that leads us to betray, others and ourselves."

Tarryn turned and wiped tears from her face. I had struck close to the mark. "Sooner or later," I concluded, "you will see my words are true."

Suso pushed for separation; he had never trusted her. I, on the other hand, saw some hope for Tarryn and chose for her to remain our guide, perhaps at our peril.

"Very well," Suso relented, "but I am convinced we will suffer for it."

"Suffering is not bad if it can bring about the deliverance of a soul." I replied. "Tarryn will be ignorant of any evil she participates in until her eyes are opened; whereupon she will feel the full weight of her oblivion."

It was time for us to move. Tarryn led us into the fog of Te Ngawah, through the Marshlands, past the Melts, and up the slopes of the Rumbling Ranges where the sun refused to shine. These mountains deserved their name; the icy slopes wore a cloak of dark and turbid cloud; the rain was heavy, the thunder growling, and rocks were falling; the very ground resented our presence. Tarryn, increasingly disturbed, nevertheless accurately guided us to a gorge named Te Atapo, The Shade of the Night. Te Atapo cut a narrow corridor through The Rumbling's shoulders to the northern face. It was a foreboding passage absorbing all who entered its miserable depression. My leg began to ache as we approached.

"This way," Tarryn explained, "I know of no other. Once only have I been through this pass. I know what awaits us there, and fear for my life."

I enquired about her previous passage. Her response was tremulous, cautious, as though fearing she might awake some dread horror. "I was young, just a girl, when my daddy carried me through, and on to the Forgotten Mountains. Though I saw the darkness, and its effect upon others who travelled with us, for some strange reason, it did not touch me."

"It is fear within that threatens you. A child in her father's arms is safe and need not fear. Look to me, Tarryn, not to the shadow, and you will emerge without harm."

"And what makes you think you can enter The Shades of the Night and remain unscathed?" Her voice was angry and shrill.

"I was old and am now young; I have been to hell itself, where I fought and defeated the shadow-beast. Now follow me."

I led the way into darkness, Tarryn close behind, with Suso at the rear. Reluctantly, we carried flaming torches; for not even my enhanced vision could penetrate Te Atapo. There would be little likelihood of undesirables observing the glow. From the moment we entered a heavy blanket was cast over us.

If Suso felt the murksome gloom, he showed little sign of it; Suso was a warrior. Tarryn struggled, terrified by creaks and howls and stalking shadows which ravaged her sporadically; whereupon I would enter the fray and gather Tarryn in my arms until the beasts retreated and her fits abated. As for me, the dagger slicing through my calf threatened to hinder; it called upon me to limp, but I refused.

As we approached the egress, Suso drew attention to the blood seeping from my leg, but I paid it no heed; it was blood well spent; the reminder of a great victory.

We emerged from the chasm. Tarryn's arms wrapped tightly round my neck, until Te Atapo's disposition was felt no more.

Suso looked to attend my leg but there was nought to be tended; the blood had vanished.

From the northern slopes we surveyed the final leg of our northern trek. Our eyes longed to behold the promised relief of The Rift, where the expansive forest of Fâwn lay between The Rumblings and the Forgotten Mountains. But instead of green, we were confronted with desolation, a barren wasteland. Every tree, every blade of grass, all flora was burned asunder. That ancient valley had lost the life it was famous for; decreated and destroyed; vitality deposed by a vicious force.

"A dragon has done this!" Suso asserted.

"Is it like a dragon to burn everything with absolute disdain for life?" I questioned.

"Dragons do not usually burn indiscriminately." Suso replied.

Tarryn soberly instructed, "Years after Rochel took the throne a dragon arose descending upon every habitation that previously prospered during Celorn's reign. It set the world on fire. Eventually its wings folded under the Forgotten Mountains."

"Nemesis has returned." Suso affirmed.

"Why has he not been dealt with?" I argued angrily. "Is there no dragon slayer in all of Moranor?"

"He is Rochel's pet." Tarryn's anxiety mushroomed. "Now you know what lies lurking in the Forgotten Mountains; now is your opportunity to turn back. Turn back now, and preserve your life."

My smile was pitiful as I instructed Tarryn to lead on; but I cautioned her, "Be careful to avoid the dragon's lair. I fear it not. You fear for good reason."

CHAPTER 26

Tarryn's Treachery

Scouring of The Rift elevated our expedition's vulnerability; whether on those gambolling hills or that raked plain we would be perilously exposed to any sinister eye. Caution was essential. From the heights we could make out a distant road that dissected the barren landscape east to west; there was no movement upon it. Tarryn directed our attention to a river that ran north from The Rumbling Ranges, and suggested that there meandered our safest route to the road.

Unlike the southerly aspect, The Rumbling's northern slopes received little precipitation and the river was virtually dry. Day and night we ran along that desiccated riverbed, stopping only when Tarryn grew weary. We ate Atlantean food, and drank the bitter water that occasioned our course.

Several days into The Rift, Tarryn disappeared. We awaited her return but she didn't show.

"She's up to no good." Suso judged.

"She could have struck trouble." I suggested, my voice betraying doubt. "We dare not call out, but we must look for her. She may be hurt. Or something worse."

Suso and I circuited the area. After several hours we could linger no longer and decided to resume our quest at a faster pace. We required little rest and sought even less than we required. That would prove our undoing. Four nights after Tarryn disappeared, it was my watch. Too late did I realise how tired I was. I awoke with a sword at my throat. Suso lay a stone-throw away covered in blood; motionless. I looked at my captors; there were at least sixty, big and dim-witted all of them. Then appeared a figure in contrast, astute, lithe and obviously feminine. I recognised who it was and burned my disappointed eyes into her culpable soul. Tarryn refused to look in my direction, but made for the leader of the mob, "I have fulfilled my vow and brought to you the fallen prince." She spoke from a cold heart; cold, but not yet callous. "Now honour the word of your masters and return to me my daughter." The foolish girl thought evil would honour a deal cut in dishonour.

She who betrayed heard the guttural voice of her betrayer pronounce doom, "Y'r daughter'd be dragon food b'now. As soon you will be." He signalled one of his men to grab her.

"Run Tarryn!" I yelled. Lost in disbelief, she could not hear my call.

Her hands quickly bound; Tarryn was shoved from brute to beast, till their leader spoke up, "Hey, enough o' that! The dragon don't want 'is food bruised." She fell to the ground and was left to lie in self-induced desolation, while attention was focused upon me.

"The fallen prince o' Moranor." He spat. "Fanks to you, wiv bin 'eld up in this god f'saken land fer free mumfs. *Free mumfs!* Each day m'boys 'ave bin pick'ns fer the dragon. And I'm gonna make you pay fer every one I lost. D'yer 'ear?"

I sought for some sign of life in Suso's languid form. The commander saw my concern and smirked, "Don't worry about 'im any longer; didn't even 'ava chance to wake up, did 'e? Passed strai' from dream t'nightmare, 'e did."

"You were fortunate you didn't wake him." I retorted. "Otherwise, all of you would be facing the void."

"Well, that we'll neva know. Will we now? What we do know is that you's two are Nephilim bound. Rochel 'as ordered yer 'ead on a platta." He gave a crowing laugh. "But first I'm gonna make yer pay f'mak'n me 'unt yer down." I glimpsed a lump of wood heading toward my face; and then, oblivion.

Consciousness returned, but I couldn't breathe; I was face down in a stagnant pool. Suddenly my head was jerked back by the hair; I spat out water and gulped down oxygen. One of the captain's goons spoke up, "Y'might 'ave gone too far, Luga; 'e ain't breav'n no good. An' y'know what them Nephilim are like. They may not leave much alive, but they 'ate receiv'n gifts that're dead."

"Check 'im out, Rawl." Luga growled.

After passing a rough examination, Rawl responded, "He's alright. A broken rib, or two. That's all. It'll be two weeks till we reach Tel Tzafit. He'll be through the worst of it by then."

Luga grabbed my collar and hoisted my face till our eyes were level. I saw a man regressed, who survived by animal instinct, empowered by beastly obsession, all fire and anger, fear and terror. I smiled and tore the splits in my lips, and tasted blood. He hurled out words of uncontrollable frustration, hate bulging with horror, "You just make sure yer don't slow us down, that's all. I don't want to spend one more night than I 'ave to in this stink'n, burned out 'ole."

Tarryn was slung over brutish shoulders whilst I was pushed to my feet and forced to run. They left Suso's body to the beasts. I lamented my friend's passing; blamed myself for it. Also, I vowed vengeance upon Luga.

CHAPTER 27

The Hungry Dragon

Scurrying along the river bed, pushed and shoved, pulled and dragged, carving tracks in silt and gravel, which returned, in kind, upon our flesh; Not till light inscribed the horizon did the pack of miscreants grind to a halt and allow us respite. Two thugs stood guard over Tarryn, another two over me. Their presence was unnecessary: Tarryn was completely dispirited; and, so long as Luga was bearing me toward my objective, I had no thought of taking leave. Not only that, the beating I endured had effectively drained every remnant of strength from my body; my eyes closed with little resistance.

A wave of fire rushed across an ocean red. I heard its awful surging, heaving and crashing; and always the pounding of The Universal Anvil. I woke up, cold and sweaty; fever was waging war against my body. I would be no good for running that day.

The flames were fanned for hours, days, perhaps weeks. Occasionally, I would stir as Tarryn's tender hand mopped my fiery head, or to jostling and hustling along the riverbed, me on a bier, as though one of the dead. Quickly, my eyes would roll and return me to the vision of fire. Once I saw Luga's brutish face sputtering a chaotic, *"I told you not to slow us down!"* The fool! In afflicting me he punished himself.

When we reached the East-West highway I surfaced from the boiling ocean. The mountains were near; between them and the highway, there ran a river, The Metaxu. We turned east, for Tel Tzafit, the Nephilim's city sepulchre. Neither Luga nor his gorillas were keen on entering that malignant mausoleum. They were torn, frayed by fear; frightened of arriving, terrified of not.

Tarryn also was scared; not only had she lost her family; she'd sacrificed her soul. It was I who she betrayed; it was I to whom she was indebted. Would she could believe there was no recrimination within me. People will sell their souls for less honourable things than family. Mine, I sold for vanity! I addressed her, "Tarryn, do not despair. I escaped the inescapable; light and love entered my hell and engraced me. Do not think I will let you wallow long in those chambers. Have hope, and know this: When facing the fire, only that which can burn gets consumed. Eventually you will understand that God never abandons us."

Tarryn gave no response: She was in Limbo!

Luga cracked the whip and his renegade machine, with Tarryn and me in tow, drove onward. With the mountains so close, I began to look for an opportunity to break free from this unsolicited and undesirable company. Luga and his buffoons lacked intelligence; they relied on brawn and animal instinct. So, I was confident that at the necessary moment I would be able to make good my escape; but first I had to awaken Tarryn from her dark night; for her sake, and mine. For, as yet, I knew not the way to Ruâch. Access to her heart may be sealed, but I didn't need to get that far, her mind would do. Should she care enough to assist me, it would prove that remnants of life and love survived in her crypt. It so happened that the task of rousing Tarryn was done for me. Getaway arrived the following day.

Nemesis must have been getting peckish, or perhaps idle curiosity roused him from his den. Whatever the cause, he found need to investigate The Rift, and so our movements upon that charred scape came to his attention. A shadow circled over us, and over, and over. High above, quietly, effortlessly, the dragon descended vulture-like, for a kill. Twenty feet above, the flying furnace exhaled a mortifying sound. A dozen or so human torches spontaneously combusted; they went running and rolling and screaming until the flame completed its work. With the force of a hurricane, the dragon swooped upon us; it brought back nightmare memories of Nehushtan. Nemesis plucked two into the air and hurled them from the clouds; one hit the ground and bounced, the other was impaled on a blackened stump. Luga's herd lacked discipline; panic rushed through the rabble and they scattered; but on that charcoal plane there was no hiding, and the dragon did its worst. It was then that Nemesis spied Tarryn, and instantly craved her tender flesh. He flew past, and passed again, leering, lusting; finally alighting before her inert frame. Until that moment Tarryn's stupor prevented her from responding to anything, but the sight of that dragon, looking, desiring, craving, cracked the shell of her coma and she screamed. Nemesis enjoyed the shrill and advanced, feasting upon her fear.

The scattering of the guards had knocked my face into the dirt, where I remained, until Tarryn's shriek drew my attention. I picked myself up and ran between Tarryn and the beast. Nemesis saw me coming, and momentarily looked to dispatch me; but surprisingly, he faltered. Time ground to a halt when into that dragon's mind, a memory that desperately he wanted to keep buried under mountains of corruption and malevolence, a memory terrible in its violence, rushed from the void and filled the terror with terror. Hesitation turned to horror. I was armed with nothing but my nerve, and it was enough to put the dragon to flight. I watched Nemesis wing it toward the highest peak.

No one else saw what transpired. Luga and his stooges lay with their heads buried in the sand. This was my moment. I turned to Tarryn and spoke with calm authority, a word that brought her hysterics to an end. Then I questioned, "Tarryn, do you know the way to Ruâch, Master of the Sword?" Her response had me surmising the possibility she was traumatised and stupefied, for instantly Tarryn revisited a childhood memory. "In the games we'd play as children," she spoke as though entranced, "if anyone was caught breaking one of the rules, we'd all chime in:

> *Deep in the mountains*
> *Where the dragon sleeps*
> *The Master and the Maker*
> *Will always play for keeps*
> *He'll come and take you by the hand*
> *He'll turn you around and around again*
> *And when He's done a sword will come*
> *To deal with all the cheats*

Daddy chastised me if he ever heard me sing it, *'There's more truth to those rhymes than you realise!'* he'd say." Tarryn laughed a little girl's laugh that quickly faded into oblivion.

I knew our window in time was lapsing; we had to make our move before Luga pulled himself, and his goons, together. I grasped her hand, "Come Tarryn, we've an opportunity to escape." However, despair had reclaimed its hold and sucked her into its pit. I pulled but she was unforgiving. Though not fully recovered from recent beatings, I gathered myself and hoisted her over my shoulder; and in so doing discovered I had strength enough bear her. Together we loped away.

The Metaxu was not far from the highway. Her waters flowed directly from the Forgotten Mountains; it ran cold and hard. The river's edge was hidden from view by a ridge. We jumped, and slid down the bank, right onto some of Luga's frightened and feckless felons who had sought refuge from Nemesis' fury. In the ensuing flurry I was knocked off balance and The Metaxu claimed me. In an instant I was swept way beyond their reach. They didn't bother giving chase, but watched till I was out of sight.

Tarryn was not so fortunate. I saw those rough and merciless hands drag her back towards Luga.

CHAPTER 28

Paradise Revisited

The Metaxu's flow sliced through me like icy daggers. I went with the current, inching toward the other side. Two leagues downstream, I crawled out of the water, bashed, bruised, and three quarters drowned. Immediately, I pushed my way along the northern bank, confident Luga would think me drowned. That side of the river had been spared Nemesis' inferno; the foliage was dense enough to conceal me from evil eyes. Further, I doubted Luga's chances of crossing the Metaxu's rapids. So, with damp confidence, I spent the day following the river, till I reached the base of the Forgotten Mountains.

Resident in every soul is an empty place that is full of longing, longing which demands fulfilment. Invariably such emptiness is interpreted as a penetrating exterior force; we think this a lonely and cruel world, or perhaps a God-forsaken life; and is none more evident than when we find ourselves in remote abandoned places, the Forgotten Mountains of this world, where forsaken feelings easily merge with the landscape. Suso was gone! Now, through my own carelessness, I had lost Tarryn. I was alone! Having grown accustomed to company, the unexpected awareness of sudden isolation began its dawn even at dusk. Here at the base of mountains, vast and impenetrable, cold and demanding, peaks piercing the seamless sky, their roots the foundations of the earth, I found myself intimidated; a silent scream was conjured in my soul, reverberating its evolving requiem against the tranquil sea of my serenity, smacking my body like waves slapping a drifting boat.

Through that immeasurable night I trudged, until despondency forced my head to lay beside the river and drown my awful solitude in sleep.

A gentle hand caressed my face. "Eden?" I welcomed, and opened my eyes. It was not Eden, nor was it Monét, nor even Tarryn. With a delightful, but disturbed, chorus of surprise my eyes rested upon the seduction of Lilith.

"Hello my love." The music of her voice was lovelier than I remembered.

"Eve, too long has been our parting." With all the suddenness of crashing cymbals, I realised how much a part of me she was, and how dearly I longed for her presence.

"I have been here always," she reassured me in her soothing, alluring, mellow manner.

No longer could I feel the cold mountain air. I looked and beheld The Metaxu altered, its rapid cut and thrust was now a lazy meander bordered by a tropical lush, a rainbow painted across an azure sky, those cold mountains were far, far away. I was in paradise. I had been here before, and knew I was in grave danger.

"Take care my love." Eve cooed; her voice as soft as summer's breeze. "Have some care for yourself. I am here to make you happy, so very happy; should you want me to stay?"

She kissed me; an ardent, lingering kiss that went in search for my soul. And Eve found me wanting.

Bliss was in my hands and I was in the hands of her. The quest felt like a fantasy. I did not know if I could find Ruách. I didn't know where He was, or if He even existed. I could be throwing my life away on a wild goose chase. At hand was my opportunity to embrace, and be embraced, by sheer bliss, and that without climbing the mountain, without suffering.

The argument racing through my mind was blindingly persuasive, yet it was met and countered by a nagging urge that advocated integrity, an urge that demanded its own claim upon my soul. '*Stop!* before you cannot!' Bliss would mean forever relinquishing the inner tranquillity that had infused my life since escaping the dungeon. Already in that kiss a portion of the peace I had grown accustomed to was wrung from me; and in that extortion I both thrilled, and quaked. '*Stop!* before you cannot.'

My emptiness desired to rest in that place; barrenness longed to own this moment of self-indulgence, it wished to fill itself with *Illusion!* I shuddered as truth became apparent; and with truth's arrival Eve's apparition faltered temporarily into transparency. Would I become transparent permanently? Would I forgo the substantiation of life? '*Stop!* before you cannot.'

I could not deny my longing for company; Suso, Monét, Tarryn, even Luga's attendance would be a more attractive proposal than being all alone. I longed for Eden, for Uriel, for The Most-High. Yes, The One! He is what my soul truly desires; He who is All and in all. That still small voice began to resonate and strengthen. The deep longing within man cannot answer its own call; it must find the answer in the depths of The Absolute.

I turned my back on Eve, whose eyes grew mournful in the parting, and woke to the bitter chill of mountain air.

Uriel had taught me the Chimaera is a nothingness which through pretension grants the illusion of being. In that waking moment I realised that not only was Eve promising false satisfaction, but desire itself was distorted, stained by my emptiness, misshapen and malformed by desperation. Genuine desire would have me filled with *Something*; the lie would fill me with nothing. The lie seeks to furnish my vacant hole with vapour. All sins are attempts to fill the void. The temptation to satisfy my emptiness with Eve, with Lilith, so strong and compelling, would lose me my mind and soul. Accepting the illusion would ensure instant satisfaction for desire distorted, whilst immediately relinquishing the opportunity and necessity for desire to be made right, and with it the prospect of becoming right myself, undistorted, to lose my stoop, to reach my full stature as a man. Why satisfy my soul eating the crumbs that fall from Chemosh's table when the food of the gods is set before me? I chose to feed on the will of The Most-High. If the mountain was for me then I will make it my food; I will devour it. If that means suffering, then I will drain the cup; and I will do it alone; for how could anyone eat food or drink wine on my behalf.

For five days I pushed on through difficult terrain, the gradient gradually rising, until, reaching The Metaxu's derivation, I could no longer hide in the valley and was forced to climb. Which I did; one mountain after another, every one appearing as though it were the tallest, until scaling each summit revealed that frozen crown possessed even higher peaks. Finally, upon a clearing morn, I emerged from a cleft and saw the dragon flying high above bearing breakfast in his claws. I saw him land and disappear into his hole. Only one more mountain to negotiate, and if Tarryn's childhood rhyme held truth, I would locate Ruâch *'where the dragon sleeps.'*

Three days later I was looking upon Nemesis' lair.

CHAPTER

The Acies Mentis

Scattered carcasses from Nemesis' slayings decorated the entrance to his cave. I harboured no heroic inclinations toward dragon slaying, so I picked my path quietly, and cautiously through the slaughter. As it happened, I saw blood and bones aplenty, but no beast. It seemed Nemesis had flown the coop. I thought this an unlikely place to find a Sword-Master.

There were three tunnels leading from the main lair; one inclining steeply; another full of rottenness so rank I doubted any living thing could be found therein; and a third, narrow, dark, and descending. As I pondered the choice before me, from behind, the faintest noise demanded investigation, for it was the muffled moan of humanity. Tethered by ropes to a charred post, a feminine form was regaining consciousness. I stepped a little closer, recognition dawning; It was Tarryn. I motioned to minister aid, and as I did a brutal roar filled the air. Nemesis had been spying and was enraged by my interest in his prize. In that same instance Tarryn's eyes opened and saw the violent torrent advancing from the rancid tunnel. Her scream echoed through the thin mountain air. I stood my ground between Tarryn and the murderous hulk. I was unafraid. Once again, mnemonic recognition caused the dragon to falter, and his violent advance ground to a bewildered halt.

"No need to be afraid." It was a voice that posed familiarity. From the shadows a lone figure entered the stage.

"Suso?" I proclaimed; doubting even as I said his name, for it did not feel like Suso, there was no light in that voice, no joy. 'He could be Suso's spectre,' I thought. Whoever, or whatever, he was, it was neither to me, nor Tarryn that he spoke, but the dragon. Dismissing my significance except in so far as I pertained to his beastly interest, he spoke with commanding tenderness, entreating the dragon as a father would his child, "Do not be afraid, he is but a man. Set your flame on him and you will see."

Nemesis obeyed, reared his fearsome head, and bellowed a deafening roar. As his sulphurous breath reached me, the air ignited, and flame coiled all around; it was dark, like the flame of Chemosh's dungeon. Though I felt heat, I did not burn. But I heard Tarryn scream; a scream that began in alarm and finished in agony, for the inferno's flaming tongues directed toward me lapped also at her flesh.

Though I wished to attend her, I had to keep my eyes upon the enemy. Its nightmare recurring, the dragon was sent in a spin. He tried once more, filling the air with his blaze. I remained, without so much as a hint of smoke clinging to me. Nemesis, took a step back, and then another; cowering and confused, he retreated slowly into his cave.

I swivelled toward Tarryn, alight at the stake. A slashing sword shredded the air on its way towards my head, as the dragon's benefactor sought to do that which his pet could not. However, before any injury could be inflicted, the blade was met with firm defence, the familiar ring of steel striking steel. I looked to see my advocate's identity, "Suso, you *are* alive!" This time there was no doubt, Suso had saved me.

What strange occasion, what horror and delight, elation and fascination, confusion and conviction; there was no time to assimilate all the information, the contrasting and conflicting emotion. I could feel the atmosphere palpably alter; the mountain air swelled and constricted becoming thick as blood and heavy as sorrow. Into it the spectre whose voice soothed the dragon, spoke, "Well met brother. Good to see you after all these years."

I gave the one speaking closer inspection. He looked like Suso, but his words were empty and upon his chest he wore the sign of a red serpent, a serpent that coiled around his body, moving and shifting, watching and whispering.

Suso urged me, "Go now, and find the Master of the Sword."

I was still caught up in the wonder and fascination of my friend's return. Suso raised the intensity of his direction, "Far be it for me to command your action, but you have come here to find Ruâch, have you not?"

I responded, "We need to help Tarryn?"

"Nothing can save her from the dragon's breath. Go!"

"I know not the way."

"Yes, you do. The narrow way, always choose the narrow way. Go now! I'll take care of things here."

Yes, I did know the way. Pushing aside every divergent urge to remain with my friend, I re-entered the cave. Unsighted pungency identified the dragon's close proximity. I plunged past the reek and through the narrows.

Down I went, deep below the dragon's lair, down to the roots of the mountain, past cold and into heat, down to the foundations of the earth where all things are pre-historic, down to the *Acies Mentis*, where there is no day yet all is aglow with innate life. The deeper I went, the deeper I became; what I did was happening in me.

Music was rumbling through the chamber bearing words that cannot be uttered. It was an infinite sound, the music that upholds the universe, universally missed by those shallow contenders for mere existence of the surface kind, but undeniable here at the core, the centre of life on earth.

I was led, by a deep call within, to a place where all is still; to The Silence where The Unstoppable meets The Immoveable. It surrounded me. Wind was somehow generated in that place; it evolved into a mighty gale. Nevertheless, I remained in The Silence, The Eye of the Storm. To step out of The Silence would be doom. There I remained. There would be no point in saying how long I remained, for time did not exist in that place.

The centre of that storm enlarged, and into that dilated eye walked a man whose single eye bespoke the sagacity of creation. His face was bright, as a newly formed star, playful and grave, affirming and disarming. He came directly to me and looked into my soul, "Well done, young prince. I am The One you seek. It is for the making that you are here. Come then, and we will make what we can of you."

I spoke not a word, not because I had nothing to say, but because there was too much to say, yet no words to say it.

Ruâch led me through the storm to The Genesis, the origin of life, where fire and metal and power combine to form all things that matter in the universe, "Here, the elements of creation find their source: Earth, Spirit, Fire, Time, Space. Here, the Song is sung and The Word is spoken. Here, all things are held together, and from here, things are torn apart."

Steel was placed in a smelter, withdrawn, and pounded with a golden hammer. Lightening flashed through the air, and thunder clapped; and the steel was thrust back into the flames. With each blow, words were spoken, unrepeatable and irrepressible. I could hear them, loud, booming, commanding. They came to me, not through the ear, but from within - and they rattled me to the core. He spoke the name of God into that sword, and, though I was not yet able to hear it, he spoke my own name. And those words fashioned me, were one with me. Somewhere in those words I became the steel in Ruâch's hands: The hammer pounded through *me and* the flames rolled over me like a great wave. Unlike the dragon's breath this flame burned, and I felt it. It took hold of my nature, melted it, and undid it. Previously, I assumed my undoing was accomplished in Uriel's tower, but this was of a different order, this was for steel, the steeling of my being, not the reclaiming of my heart; here was the shaping and sharpening of my life. This mystery saw my harrowing dream fulfilled; and it proved worse than the portent.

The steel was beaten and forged, beaten and forged. The operation was replicated until the metal was virtually transparent: I was completely undone. Next came the folding; folding, and more beating, and more fire. Ruâch paused, fixed His eye on mine, transfixed: "Fire for purity! The hammer for strength!" He declared, and resumed the regimen.

An eternity elapsed; yet in the end it was a quick work. When all was said and done, Ruâch let out a mighty laugh, placed the sword in my hand, and proclaimed, "Behold! Aléthéa, Sword of the King!" Then, he charged me with these words, "Be vigilant! Be strong! Remember to keep your sword sharp, for your life and rule depend on it. Keep it sharp in war, but also in peace, when men are prone to lose their edge and distinction."

I held Aléthéa and could feel her song. From my heart my mouth erupted, *"Kirith Selastur Sendemor Larushtan."* Meaning, "He who was, and was not, now is again!" And, more words I cried:

Upon those who have sat in darkness
In the land where death casts shadow
A great light now shines

CHAPTER

Ungründ's Recreation

Ruâch kept me in the belly of the earth for an age, yet when I emerged the scenario from which I parted appeared unchanged, more or less: Tarryn was smouldering at the damsel's stake, Suso, sword in hand, remained on guard before his doppelganger. One thing had altered however, the spectre had been joined by others of like kind, six in all, who stood observing the two in tension, conjoining their will together in a battle for Suso's mind.

I could feel the blood pulsing in my veins as I called out to Suso, who answered without averting his eyes from the spectre, "I thought you were on your way to the Sword Master?"

"I've been," I announced triumphantly, "and have returned!"

Suso and his foe both looked at me, "You have grown," Suso's voice was swelling with joy and surprise, "and you are luminous." Something not missed by the Nephilim, who were rippling under threat.

Suso's rival assessed the situation's gravity and with rising urgency attempted to broker a deal, "Come, join us, brother. If you do, we will leave your friend intact for another day."

Suso's voice was stern in reply, "Neither you, nor your reptilian connections, will lay one blow upon him, for I am charged with his safekeeping."

"Very noble, little brother, but not very clever," the spectre's voice corrugating contempt, "Is it not time to introduce me to this *mad savage*? I would have him bow before me."

Suso winced a little, as those ill spoken words were recalled from the abyss and hurled back in his face, "Pride was your downfall, and your words betray how low you have fallen." Suso retorted. "It is for you to bow the knee, not he. Humble yourself; acknowledge him as Moranor's true king, and perchance you might save yourself from the nightmare of your own making."

"Who, or what, is this thing with which you appear acquainted?" I inquired.

"He was Vennar," Suso replied, with the slightest hint of sorrow in his voice, "My brother, who, through pride, fell to the Chimaera. He descended into emptiness and became the form you now behold. Together, the fallen seven became the Nephilim, who serve Rochel, and control the dragon in the Chimaera's absence."

"Yes, we are brothers," Vennar sneered, "but there was no fall on my behalf, it was a rising, an empowering; power I offer to you Suso. Your youthful idealism is quaint, but your quest chases the wind. Moranor is in darkness, and so it should be; only when it is dark are we truly free."

The Nephilim's words reminded me of the sophist, Dorran-ap Lusdburn, and induced such revulsion that I commanded, "Cease your meaningless words!"

The spectre's mouth continued to move, but he lost his voice.

"Come Suso;" I called, "We must help Tarryn."

"Tarryn is burned, she burns still." Suso lamented. "It's because her heart was not pure. I told you not to trust her. Leave her to the flame. It is mercy to her."

"I saw light in her darkness," I contended, "I see life in her still."

I moved towards Tarryn, and as I did the league of fiends leaped upon us. Those darkened spirits possessed no power over me; they were little more than an annoyance, all bluff and bluster. However, it was not so with Suso; they were much more real to him, especially his anti-brother, Vennar. It was for Suso's sake that I unsheathed Aléthéa. The sight of her naked blade and the song she sang sent two of the Nephilim into immediate madness, frothing and grovelling, covering their eyes, and blindly thrashing their swords. The others became incensed, erupting into multiplied levels of ferocity.

When blades first joined and jarred and that steely shudder ran up my arm, it felt as though I had woken to the morning sun, as though I had leaped into a stream of living water, and that same stream began to flow from me. The spectres fought wildly, even fantastically. We reciprocated. Suso and I were avid, every blow, deliberate.

Eyes were watching. When I emerged from the narrows Nemesis fled through the upward tunnel and remained perched upon the mountain's peak from where he observed our exchange. It was when Suso and I were gaining the upper hand that he who used to be Vennar called for Nemesis' assistance. Harnessed by the Nephilim's strong directive, the dragon plummeted. The first I knew of his presence was the deafening roar that preceded the furnace's ignition. I knew what was coming and yelled for Suso to hit the ground. The Nephilim withdrew, though inhuman they still feared the dragon's fire. I fell upon Suso and protected him. Flaming tongues lashed at my body but again found nothing to burn. In his maddened rage the dragon came again, this time swooping too low; for I was on my feet, and with one slash separated wing from body. He fell to the ground, a whirling dervish, a thrashing, churning, wailing work of wickedness. I leaped to finish him off. Two Nephilim stood in my way, but they were hesitant, and hesitation proved their undoing, for Aléthéa tore through them, and they dissolved in an explosion of light. Upon the beast's shoulders, I rode roughshod, until Aléthéa descended heavily upon the armoured neck and severed it above the shoulders. Blood splattered abstractly over the earth's canvas.

With the rest of the Nephilim taking flight, Suso and I found ourselves alone. I wrapped my cloak around Tarryn, smothering the remaining flames and lifted her charred body from the burning stake. I knew not what to do. She was clinging to life, tenuous but sure.

"There is one who could help her," Suso suggested.

My heart rose in hope, "And who would that be?"

"Uriel; He alone can save her."

"Yes, but you offer vain hope, Suso. Uriel, as well you know, is not here; he walks the oceans west."

"True, but Ungründ could carry her to him."

My intention was for life to drain completely out of the dragon so its menace could never be re-invented, but here lay opportunity to redeem the dragon's wickedness. A menacing tremor lingered in Nemesis' heart, so I opened his chest, held the pulsing black offal in my hand and commanded good to come out of evil. That heart, cold and hard and vain and vile warmed in my hand and then softened, the foul stench disappeared, replaced by the aroma of fields after a spring shower. A burst of brilliance silenced the dread beat, and from the light Ungründ was manifest in all his glory. We draped Tarryn's body over his back and summoned him to bear her to the Old Man of the Sea. Ungründ parted upon a carpet of golden rain, cleansing us, and the mountain, of all dragon filth.

CHAPTER 31

The Absolução

Suso slapped me on the back, "We could go a hundred years and not have such a remarkable reunion. Now let me look at you: By Uriel's beard, you are a sight to behold; much taller than before, and your face radiates like lapis lazuli under a full moon."

"I have been purged by the wave of fire, strengthened under Ruâch's golden hammer, de-created and recreated, deformed and reformed. Much more, I have an oath to fulfil: I must bring an end to Moranor's oppression and let this fair land taste spring again." I knew not from where the oath had come; I must have received it implicitly in the making of the sword.

"Then, where to, my lord?" Suso's enthusiasm was inspired

"Suso, we are friends, and I deem myself in debt to you, so faithful have you been to this mad savage. It does not feel right for you to take direction from me. Should you wish to remain with me, I would be most grateful, but you are free to follow your heart. For my part, I must go to the Fields of Death, wherever they be. The Nephilim have surely flown straight to Rochel to inform him of my presence, and the plight of his pet. Meanwhile, he amasses an army to war against me. And I will withstand him!"

"Many leagues south, and east from here, where the Acheron River slows to a gentle flow, the planes are known as the Fields of Death. They have been called that since the days of treason. There, the bravest of Moranor were slain and left to rot." Suso's voice was grave and committed. "I have felt destined to return there since my youth. There's something in the soil of that place; you can feel the battle endures. Take me with you, my lord, and consider me yours to command."

My face portrayed fortitude tinged with anxiety, "You are worth an entire regiment, I have no doubt; but the two of us alone would find Rochel's hordes too large to handle."

"Well, I could handle a thousand," Suso boasted. "Together, we'd best ten thousand. Any more and we may need some help."

"There will be more - of that you can be assured." My voice was grim, but Suso laughed as best he could; and it was infectious. It felt good to laugh again.

"Then let us make our way to the Planes of Acheron, my lord, and see who The One invites to our quest."

We descended the Forgotten Mountains, far beyond the eyes of Tel Tzafit. From there, The Rift, though narrowing, continued through to the Acheron River. During our trek Suso related his return from death: After Luga's goons had bludgeoned him, a wave of oblivion overwhelmed Suso: he considered himself dead. Indeed, for a time he walked with souls deceased and departed; he saw the army of warriors who ride their chariots across the sky, and would have joined them but for Uriel's voice, which glided on the wind, commanding, "Not yet Suso. I charged you to look after the king, now you must fulfil your duty." In that same moment Monét was dispatched. She came upon Suso's body and bore it back to Eden, where he was healed with leaves from the Tree of Life.

I should have asked Suso how he was able to travel the distance from that fairest of lands in time to save my skin. I should have asked how is it that his brother, being of the same noble blood as Suso, could possibly fall from grace.

Instead, I teased, "I declare Suso, on our parting from Eden, Monét could not keep her eyes off you." And then I added, "Though she was not impressed by me one whit."

Suso's smile revealed a measure of discomfort, "Forgive Monét's abrupt manner my lord, we are pledged to be married. She is angry that I am charged with your wellbeing, for I cannot make good my vow to her until your kingdom is restored."

"Aha! Now I understand." I smiled. "She has done nothing that requires pardon. I would ask forgiveness of her: It is my failure that has forced your separation, for had I not fallen the world would be a different place, and you would not feel beholden to me. As for your marriage, I release you from your pledge. Go, with my blessing, and marry your love." Try as I might to persuade him, Suso refused to accommodate any notion of our parting.

We travelled many days, keeping well away from the road, encountering neither man nor beast, until we arrived where the great river finds her source. It was there, where the Forgotten Mountains reach their end, and the Rumbling Ranges begin, that we spied a thin tower of smoke rising high above the plain.

That smoke belonged to a company of soldiers, no more than eighty strong. For some time, we observed. They bore little similarity to Luga and his bounty hunters, being more orderly and far less barbaric. They camped under a white banner bearing a golden chalice brimming with red wine. Suso suggested avoidance. I understood his caution; we had become accustomed to covert operations; but the time for secrecy had passed, "If they are our enemy, we will have to face them some time, Suso, either here, or on the Fields of Death. Better when they are few in number than combined with Rochel's multitudes. Yet, I think good fortune resides here, for I detect a noble bearing in their ranks. Perhaps we might find some friends among them."

We stole right into their camp without detection. Our word of greeting brought their communion to an abrupt end. Talk, laughter, and food fell from their mouths. A ring of swords immediately surrounded us. They were unaccustomed to being interrupted at meal.

These soldiers were tall, though shorter than Suso, and thick set. Their uniform was blue and silver. A voice spoke out of the crowd, according to Suso, in the native style of the north, Navarian by idiom, Sorrentine by accent, "These are not days for strangers to be paying casual visits uninvited." The circle of swords opened to reveal a quirky, youthful character, with two very wary warriors by his side. "You are either brave, desperate, or foolhardy; and I would place my bet upon the latter," the young one declared.

"Foolishness lies in deed, but is oft revealed through word. Foolish indeed is the man who would wager upon such vast alternatives as have been suggested," I replied. "As it is we fit none of your categories, though foolish and desperate we may seem. We are here as friends, or foes, depending upon the character of those before whom we stand. With me is Anselm, son of Aneurin the Invincible and Aurelia Daughter Immaculate; he is Suso to those who know him well. I would tell you my name if I knew it, but so far it is kept from me. What I do know I will tell: my father's name is Celorn the Sublime, and my mother, Gwenlorra Daughter Immaculate. Now, who am I addressing sir, that I may know whether you are deserving respect, for so far you have earned yourself little more than derision."

Amidst the din that followed, the youthful voice advanced, "So, it is true, the fallen one has returned."

"I judge not the integrity of strangers," spoke one of the wary, "Especially one who claims to have returned from the place where no man escapes. You could be Saba's suckling for all we know!" He spouted. "Yet Suso is a name known to be valiant, borne by one who has no peer in peace or war. If it be Suso who stands before us we have honourable company indeed."

"I am Suso; and you may say of me whatever you will, but speak against my lord at your peril; for I am pledged to guard him with my life."

"Proof will be required," demanded the wary. "Show us your mark."

Cautiously Suso removed his coat and shirt, revealing a torso painted with all manner of imagery. Etched into his left arm was the picture of a snake, like the one worn by Vennar. Except this one was incomplete, headless; the snake hanging motionless, in the grip of an invisible hand.

Noise erupted all around. The young one laughed, "Suso, Suso, Suso; well met indeed." Wary countenances relaxed. "I ask no pardon over precaution; these are terrible times. But I am honoured to set eyes upon you, and he who you deem fit to serve."

The quirky character chimed, "I am Evagrios, commander of The Absoluçion, Sorrentas' Legionnaires. He who vouches for Suso's reputation is Cassian, and on my left, is Arrelay. They are my closest friends and two of the bravest warriors you will have the pleasure to meet." A roar of approval went up from the surrounding soldiers. "And The Absoluçion, with whose swords you are acquainted, is more dedicated, more skilled, and more edifying than any regiment I have ever served." Loud endorsements confirmed their mutual appreciation.

"Dedicated to who or what?" Suso inquired.

"Why, dedicated to ourselves, loyal to one another. What could be more appropriate during these days of treachery!?"

"There is only one who deserves absolute loyalty," I interjected. "Without devotion to The One, loyalty degenerates to self-interest."

"Yes! Yes! Yes! We all serve The Most-High here. Yet, if the young prince had been more loyal to his father's kingdom, Rochel would never have taken the throne." Evagrios was wilier than impressions first indicated.

"I remember little of those days; my failure was a lack of substance, an issue of integrity. Loyalty is possible only when one has fidelity. I sense you Absoluçion have a certain common dependence; loyalty enough for one another, as long as it is mutually beneficial. But true loyalty abounds in love, and springs from conviction, from truth; serving the truth in love."

Arrelay, growing increasingly uncomfortable with our tête-à-tête, spat, "What truth?"

I did not take my eyes off Evagrios for I wished him to make a decision, "Why, the truth that sets all mankind free; the truth that would rid this land of tyranny; the truth that you, and all Moranor, should live, to enjoy sun and rain without fear of shadow."

"But we are free!" Evagrios assured with a chuckle. "Rochel lives far from Sorrentas and bothers us little; and he has vowed to leave things as they stand in exchange for a little boundary riding and information."

Suso's suspicion again butted in, "What kind of information?"

"Well, for instance, he would be very interested that we have bumped into you."

Suso reached for his sword.

"There will be no need for your sword Suso," Evagrios' laughed. "I said he would be interested; I did not say I would tell him. I have no liking for Rochel; I simply have a liking for life, and the lives of those under my care; which at this moment includes you. You will join our meal, and tonight rest in peace; nothing will threaten you inside the circle of our brotherhood."

"We will accept your offer." I concurred; though Suso was not so receptive. "May you accept mine? When morning comes you and your men join us. We ride for the Fields of Death."

Evagrios' smile withered into worry, "You are riding into a storm; we won't go there. We will not go where angels dare not tread. No-no-no-no-no-no! We will wait! And should The Most-High give you back your throne, you will find us willing allies."

"I fear if you do not come, you may not be found at all."

Finding the conversation too incisive, Evagrios forced a little false laughter and called for food, "Let this moment be a small respite in your difficult journey. We will enjoy our time together and see what the morning brings."

CHAPTER 32

Blind Justice

In the bowels of night, Evagrios woke us, all earnest and urgent, "Arise my friends, the day approaches and treachery with it. Distance you must put between us before the sun rises and rouses the land. Your arrival has brought mischief to the boil."

Hurriedly we were informed that in the night's darkest hours, Arrelay, along with several others, slipped away; the sentinel saw them riding toward Tel Tzafit, "It proves the peril of our times when sedition can be found within The Absoluçion. That one of my closest would succumb to the enemy's subtlety is unforeseen, and gathers great grief to my heart."

The Absoluçion were admirable; they were also affable, almost to the point of flippancy. In such cavalier conditions, darkness resides with little fear or respect. "Evil comes in many forms," I associated, "the more insidious grows right under our nose."

Evagrios agreed, "Fortunately, I don't have a very large nose or the situation might have been much worse. For now, it does not help to get caught up in matters of appearance. What is necessary, is that you must fly."

Waiting in the centre of camp were nine horses, saddled with provisions. In answer to my questioning eyes Evagrios related with customary jocularity, "You are very fortunate to have stumbled upon The Absoluçion, most generous of all Moranor's militia. After you retired, Cassian approached me wishing to join your quest, wherever it may lead. His camaraderie, I will sorely miss. Rest assured he will prove his worth to you." He almost laughed, but a tear brooked the crease of Evagrios' eye, "The men know of Cassian's decision. I offered everyone the opportunity to follow his lead. The result provides you with six more of my best warriors. Our benevolence extends even further: Viola!" The reigns of several horses were placed in our hands, "Warriors of your demeanour will look more handsome mounted. Ride them valiantly. We Absoluçion value our horses as much as life itself. This is the least I can do to allay the harm Arrelay's treachery might bring your way."

Evagrios' generosity matched his charm, and I asked him to reconsider joining us. Deflecting the offer with mirth, he embraced me and sent us on our way. In that embrace I was transported to a place I had never seen before, but knew to be Sorrentas; it was under fire. Luga and men of similar menace were putting the city to the torch. Women and children were being slaughtered. I heard their screams and saw their surrender, denied. As we parted I advised Evagrios, "We will meet again, of that, I am sure. For now, return to your city, and save it if you can."

Nine of us rode south, our road taking us through the city of Avignôn. Those Absoluçion accompanying us were well acquainted with the country north of Navara. Having recently patrolled the borders of their land they were confident we would find no nefarious elements on this stretch of our journey. They were wrong.

Avignôn was Cassian's birthplace. He assured us it bore a gracious nature, and, accordingly, would welcome us with geniality. Not only that, but he was confident many enthusiasts would wish to join our fellowship. His buoyant promise was encouraging enough, yet it smacked a little romantic for my liking; as was shortly confirmed when our entry into Aviğnōn arrived uncelebrated; a cemetery would have heralded our coming with more eagerness. We quickly learned, however, that the frosty atmosphere could not be blamed upon the nature of the city, for we entered their streets barely a day after they had been attacked and ransacked.

Cassian disappeared momentarily. He returned, leading survivors from a secret shelter. Fortunately, for the women and children, forewarning bought them enough time to secure sanctuary under the city's foundations. Unnervingly, no men could be seen, for in that place no man remained alive. "Nechlor has done this," he'd already discovered, "And I'll make sure he pays with his life."

Nechlor had been commissioned by Rochel to bring his warriors and join the war. Their route passed directly across Aviğnōn's path. Entry was denied, but the invaders engaged and overwhelmed the city's defences.

Cassian seethed, "Rabid dogs! I will rid the earth of every Scad that dares enter this country."

I enquired of the petrified, "Tell me, how many were in Nechlor's army?"

A young warrior woman, spoke strongly, "Between four and five thousand; all on foot except for Nechlor. Scads have no horse skill. Horses have more sense than to put up with them."

"Then it will not prove difficult to run them down," I surmised. "We will drive them back to Scadia, or down to hell, whichever they prefer."

Suso looked at me, pleasantly surprised. "There are nine of us, Suso. According to your maths, we are more than enough for the few we will meet today."

"Make that twelve!" added the young lady, "Here are three shield-maidens whose arrows never miss their mark."

"Your services," I prescribed bluntly, "might be better served nurturing your city."

"We were prevented from defending her: No one will deny our revenge!"

"Is there not some grieving for you to undertake?" I implored. The warrior women would not relent, "Look around. Observe the faces of the women and children of Avignôn. There is enough grief here for all eternity. These all died along with their husbands and fathers. We are alive, and would best serve this city by putting an end to the plague sweeping through our land. Let the dead bury the dead. It is in honour of those whose blood floods the gutters of our streets that we would terminate the Nechlorian disease. The sooner the better!"

I remained unpersuaded; nevertheless, the shield-maidens were irresistible. So it was, that the twelve of us left the survivors of Avignôn to grieve, as they should, whilst we went to deal with the enemy, as we should.

Throughout that day we hunted Scads. The sun sank beyond the horizon, and still we chased. Several hours into the night we caught sight of their camp.

"Let's fall on them while they sleep," burst Cassian, still full of fury.

"Patience Cassian. Twelve of us there are, and I will not lose any to these pack animals, not even to a chance blow. Suso and I will pay Nechlor a visit and see if we can persuade him to lay down weapons and return to Scadia."

"That won't do. He must pay for what he has done to Avignôn. And I will make him!"

"No, Cassian, I need you here. The others know and respect you. The Most-High is the one who will ensure Nechlor pays for his crimes. Nobody gets away with anything. He will rue the day he stepped foot in your city. If it comes to a clash of arms, as I am certain it will, I need you to watch for Scads on the run. We must take every single one. Should any escape, they will become festering sores in Moranor. Surround the camp, become an impenetrable barricade, position yourselves so no man can make it through your wall."

Several large fires, impudently lit, drew soldiers like moths to the flame. As the warriors were intent on managing their comfort, it was with relative ease that we accessed the camp undetected, and sliced our own entrance into Nechlor's tent. Suso dispatched the guards to the netherworld without them making a sound. I located Nechlor and kicked him off his bed; his rotund frame cushioned the fall. Suso hushed his squeal with the point of a dagger.

"The opportunity is yours," I offered the voluminous vagrant, "to save the lives of your men. Your own is forfeit! You shall pay for the fell deeds committed against the citizens of Aviğnōn. Tell your soldiers to return to Scadia - minus their weapons of course. What say you to that, Nechlor?"

Sweat and saliva slithered down his face; rage, without courage, enflamed his eyes, "We are here to join Rochel's army, to fight a nameless and numberless foe, a phantom for all I know, a legend of prophecy. Bah! I care not for chasing the wind, but I do care that insolence has entered my chamber and threatened this king. Ten thousand of the fiercest warriors are at my call. If I were you, boy, I would fly home to your mother before you burden her with the burial of your body."

"Your girth, Nechlor, is exceeded only by your pride, and your pride spawns incomparable foolishness. Would you consign five thousand dogs to oblivion when they could return home to care for their packs?"

"Rochel has ordered me here. Their return would bring war upon my own land. No, I will not send them home."

"Then here you shall all die." I concluded.

Nechlor's face swelled as large as a pumpkin and turned wine red. From huge lips he bawled, *"Rid me these infidel intruders."*

Curtains opened and more than a dozen warriors rushed at us. Instantly, Aléthéa was at hand, her glorious blade ablaze with Almighty wrath. Lightening flashed, striking those in the tent sightless, which instead of quietening hostility, only served to incense their ravenous passion. They were thrice blind, body, heart, and mind. Blindly they swung their blades, flailing the air and each other.

Noise erupted throughout the camp. We left the tent, and those inside, to desecrate each other in frothy bloodlust. Outside, the camp almost defied description, certainly it baffled belief: The inner circle was struck with the same malady as those within the tent. Mayhem effused round and round; panic spread in every direction. The entire army fought one another in madness, their rampaging, ravaging madness. Beyond the inner circle, in defence of their own lives, soldiers were forced to fight against their blind countrymen. The Most-High had sent terror throughout the army.

It was for the perimeter that we ran, cutting a swath through their dishevelled ranks. Side by side, Suso and I dealt with all who came within reach. And in the course of that battle, a transition took place: The clashing chaotic intensity slowed to a smooth rhythmical action; the awful din retreated to the background; I heard the song and moved accordingly. On the hills above, our comrades watched in awe: they said the battle frenzy came upon us; to me there was no frenzy at all. It was then that the thousands began to run, this way and that way, slashing one another in fear fuelled fury. Our swords did not cease their singing until Suso and I stood shoulder to shoulder, victorious. We had entered the commotion but the commotion did not enter us; rather, we overcame it.

By morning's light not a Scad remained standing in that valley of blood. It should be known; more were slain by their own sword than by ours. As for Cassian, though I left him livid, neither he nor his compatriots missed the battle, for as the Scad cowards tried to desert the heat of conflict, they ran into the ferocious fire of the surrounding wall. Whilst it is possible one or two could have escaped, never again were Scad warriors seen in all of Moranor.

Nechlor was barely alive, having received scores of wounds from the blind blades of his personal protectorate. What life remained within his bubonic frame I gave to Cassian, who, together with the shield-maidens of Avignōn, beheld justice that day without destroying their souls through exacting vengeance. He cast Nechlor's regalia into the fire, and left the one he so despised to the scavenging dogs and vultures, already gathering to the field of carrion.

CHAPTER 33

The Great Beast

"Farewell, shield-maidens of Aviǧnōn." I saluted. However, our leave-taking was forestalled yet again: Forging personality into an amalgam of steel, they were resolute and passionate, single-mindedly determined to right Moranor's wrongs. I was struck by their visage: all ice and fire, deathly beautiful. There was little likelihood of persuading them to leave, and I would be a fool to try. They had proven themselves; their will and stature were worthy of true warriors. Further, they constrained all unwarranted sentimentality whilst possessing an acutely honed and responsive intuitive faculty; in other words, sensitivity. "Your desire for justice is honourable," I acknowledged, "yet, I can only promise you hardship and death."

"We face it willingly. For, as far as we judge the matter, our best chance at life lies in following you." Their jaws were set like steel.

It would be wrong to judge them as cold or heartless, these women were not like stone. Commonly, such impassion accompanies the shelving of tenderness and emotion abused by suffering endured. But these angels of Aviǧnōn embraced and embodied a femininity closely resembling the Immaculati. Assured of their place on earth and in heaven, they have become masters of their own domain.

So it was that twelve continued our venture south, entering the province of Berea; as we did, the earth rumbled. Since arriving in Moranor, Suso and I had grown accustomed to unnatural earthly phenomena; and more than once we commented such geological gyrations were increasing in frequency and intensity the further south we travelled.

Concerned that our current path was unnecessarily arduous, the shield-maidens, Kareah, Urshûah, and Serene, suggested we move closer to The Acheron and journey by way of the road to Montobora. The cultural centre of Moranor, Montobora was renowned for its riches, literary and commercial; moreover, it boasted a formidable militia; and further, furnished provisions for all Moranor's forces along the eastern border. In hope of discovering some noble warriors who might dare join us, I agreed to the suggestion. However, entering the city would necessitate shrewd vigilance for Montobora would not have avoided Rochel's attention or influence.

Hypotheticals, wondering and wishing and projecting into the future, are a waste of time and energy, so I did not inflate hope or dissipate my mind in the fanciful speculation that we would have men flocking to our cause. In fact, my gut hedged toward the very opposite: For wherever people gather, no matter the form, political, religious, or social, there have I observed The Great Beast, and the masses seated upon its back. It is The Beast that turns man into a social animal. Humanity rises to shape society, then, once shaped, reverts to the animal state. The most prolific example of our tendency to live like animals is the impulse to herd. All we like sheep have gone astray. Accustomed to living for the pleasure of this world, the instinct to accept and be accepted usurps our higher and nobler design, that of living by and for what is truly good. Instead, we consider it good to be conformed to society's expectations, whether such expectations are good or evil. In so doing we lose nobility and freedom, joy and purpose: in a word, Life.

As I had to rise and fight to escape the mire, so must all. It is a deathly journey, this waking and rising from the stupor, a constant battle for truth. Many interpret this battle as a fight for freedom, but it is not liberty for which the oppressed make war, though it may seem so at the time. What makes us really fight, in all our various and confused manner, is our desperation for justice; we yearn to bring an end to the breeching of universal law, for all that is scattered to return to The One, for chaos and anarchy to reach its conclusion, for nature to be reordered. For this, the whole earth groans, until virtue germinates and generates the restoration of order and unity in the universe: in a word, Peace. I, who had once sold my soul to darkened powers, had risen from the grave for precisely this.

Such musings accompanied me along the road to Montabora. Glimmers from the metropolis' marble buildings strobed across the horizon as the city saluted the dawn. We were not far away, five leagues at most.

Our road, constructed as it was, on the Acheron's upper plain, showed signs of previous flooding. To our left, the mellow meanders of the river were erupting with a richness of colour, cool blues, fiery reds, and burnished bronze, as the sun wrestled to break above the horizon and attempt yet again an ascent to its blazing glory.

Without notice, our horses halted; ears erect, clouds of steam snorting from flared nostrils, tension fused their flanks, they waited, suspended. We perused all angles for the cause warranting their concern. It was then I beheld a strange shimmer on the river's surface. Perhaps it was the wind? But dawn's air remained motionless. The horses threatened to bolt. Fortunately, all of us were horsemen enough to hold their will and feed them composure. Noise began rolling toward us, subterranean rumblings, the deep groan of a suffering world; I could hear it in my belly. Montobora's incandescence distorted and was eventually lost completely from sight, engulfed by a dark cloud. The mushrooming haze approached. Ahead of it, a crack was streaking like a lightning bolt toward us, dividing and serrating the road asunder. All around, the earth was heaving, and tearing, and groaning.

"This is of Rochel's making." Suso declared.

"Then we shall ride to meet it." I returned, and spurred my horse toward the fracture, Suso with me, the others behind. Within moments, the distance between us and the fissure, was spanned. The clawing chasm reached for me. I leapt from my saddle, unsheathing Aléthéa mid-flight. With my feet planted firmly on the shaking ground, I pointed my sword to the heavens and cried aloud, *"Everion Rasu La-Sundarüm."*

As those words filled the air, the ground under my feet became stronger, more solid, as if my word had gathered the ground to itself. I thrust Aléthéa into the earth; from me strength flowed, permeating the ground, engaging the jagged ripping tear, and withstanding it until the rumbling ceased, and the fracture finally halted at my feet.

Within moments the huge crevasse came alive as dark and ghastly things emerged, terrified by Aléthéa's light. They ran, crept, and slithered off into hiding. Then, slowly at first, the wound closed and the earth, for the most part, was healed.

Suso warned, "Rochel knows we march by this route."

Cassian, with customary caution, looked at the women, "Was it in innocence that you desired this road, or something more sinister?"

"Would we put ourselves in harm's way deliberately?" Urshûah retorted.

Serene added, "The suit of treachery is worn more easily by men than women, Cassian."

I smiled, for she spoke truth. Men absolve themselves of the worst deeds and desires with a shrug of the shoulders. Women, however, are not so moulded, and, with few exceptions, tend not to wear treachery well at all. I neither saw, nor felt, any deception in these shield-maidens.

Kareah, who was younger than the others, remained demure; her naivety was beyond offence, and her silence suggested the appropriate directive, "This is not helpful. I propose that we live above suspicion, and look toward the great need ahead in Montobora."

As we approached the city, my eyes spied a distant figure reigning his horse west, before disappearing over the crest of a hill.

Montobora lay in ruin; its foundations rent, buildings razed to the ground, and many trapped under rubble. The walking wounded were suffering; traumatised, they had become distant drifters, strangers in their own town. I was moved by their plight, "We have a journey to make but far be it from us to leave this city in its current state. We will remain to render whatever assistance we can."

For five days we helped bring order and healing; but the good we generated was received apprehensively, almost begrudgingly. I could see why, for lurking above the city, like a seething infestation, was The Great Beast. Generally, The Beast is content to work invisibly, shrouded in an intoxicating haze of social coalition. However, on occasion, such as this catastrophe, it was working frantically, pushing and pulling its puppets, attempting to return everything to the city's ordered estate; and always generating suspicion towards outsiders. Consequently, there was little credibility granted us by the authorities. They were proud, subtle, and embarrassed that their state of affairs obliged our assistance. Further, they rejected our notion that Rochel had worked the earthquake, preferring, in spite of their education and sophistication, a reversion to superstition. They fixed the blame in our direction, for the earthquake coincided with our arrival. Uncomfortable in our presence, they wished us gone from the moment we arrived.

But not everyone was of the same ilk. In the still of night, as we prepared to leave the city, Luhrs, commander of Montobora's armed forces, sought me out. He vowed to join us as soon as he had completed his duty and restored order. He had no liking for Rochel, or Montobora's aristocracy. In turn the collective held Luhrs in contempt. He maintained command by sheer weight of personal authority, and the overwhelming support of Montobora's populace: status he earned ten years prior by single-handedly defending the city against Nemesis and saving it from the dragon's flames.

Luhrs would have been a welcome addition to our ranks; but his solitary promise was our only escort leaving the city's fallen gates.

CHAPTER 34

Finding Evagrios

Something was wrong; I was confident that by now our ranks would have swollen. We were either out of time, or out of place; something was yet undone, or still to come. Either way, there was nothing to be done but call a halt to proceedings.

"We are no longer welcome in Montobora," I shared. "But I am bound still to this place and cannot resume our journey until my heart allows it."

We made camp not far from the city's gates.

Waiting: The tightrope suspended between patience and urgency; with-straining the onward urge with open hands but clenched teeth; poised for what I knew was sure to come. Three days passed before Beldür drew attention to a cloud of dust racing the setting sun. Riders, many riders, were heading our way. Suso cautioned us to lay low until we assessed the nature of the posse, but I could see the flag under which they rode, white with a golden chalice, the banner of The Absoluçion. My heart leaped! This was what I had been waiting for.

Evagrios arrived a changed man; gone the flippant jocularity; gone the heady *ha ha ha,* the trite *te he he* and *tra la la.* Upon his cavalier face was engraved the deaths of all whom he sought to protect; his home burned, family murdered, the city a charred pyre. The unwelcome nightmare welcomed The Absoluçion as they rode into the city of Sorrentas. It took two weeks to bury the mutilated, whereupon they rode upon a storm of revenge to join our quest.

"We will fight to the death!", Evagrios gravely assured. "We are ready to follow you now; we have no home, no family, life is gone with the passing of Sorrentas. We have existence and resentment - That is all!" Poison was erupting from his spleen. "Grant us one thing: That we will make Rochel pay for the murder of the innocent."

"Revenge will not remove your pain, my friend." With those words, I realised a transformation had taken place within me. Somewhere between Eden and this moment my intention of exacting vengeance upon Rochel had lifted, replaced by a quiet confidence that the scales of justice rested in the hands of The Highest.

Evagrios answered, "I do not seek to have the arrow extracted from my heart. I simply mean to put one through his."

"I understand your rage, and doubt not your purpose. But of one thing I must be assured, should you ride with us, you and your men must be answerable to my command."

Hostile eyes burned, yearning for accord. I returned his gaze, but not the emotion. Finally, he responded, "The Absoluçion know your destiny. We have heard the prophecy. Already yours has proven the better way. We are with you, young king, allies, and servants, if you want us. It is through you that damage will be inflicted upon the adversary. It is through you that his end will come."

"What of Arrelay?" Cassian interrupted, "I'm sure that traitor played no small part in Sorrentas' genocide." His rabid wrath proving it is easier to forgive an enemy than a friend. "I would blood him through and through were he before me."

"The turncoat still roams free." Evagrios replied.

"You will see them again," I declared. "Look for them on the Acheron Fields. Look for them among those who are like them. Evil cannot long dwell in the company of the good; the gadfly cannot soar with the eagle. Had you been less superficial, or more substantial, their exposure would have been the sooner."

"That lesson has been sorely learned; but there is also something for you to learn: We have brought with us a warrior from the south, a long-time friend who observed first-hand what is bubbling in Rochel's cauldron. He can tell you the name and number of your foe. He it is who told us where to find you."

"The lone rider." I remembered. "Let me hear his news."

"Come Nassûr," Evagrios summoned, "Come tell your future king what lies between him and his throne."

"Before you speak, Nassûr, I would say something." I raised my voice for all to hear. "There is much talk aligning myself with the throne, but it has not come from me. In all honesty the thought is beyond me. I am not worthy of title or honour, for I am the fallen. It is by grace alone that I stand at all. The Most-High rules and reigns over the nations of the world, and I am His servant, His hand in the land; and the doom of any hand that rises against His. I am that, nothing more!"

"And nothing less!" Suso interrupted, helping my words be few.

"Now, Nassur, speak," I continued. "What news of the south?"

Nassur's story was brief, and bleak. Rochel had amassed an army of more than fifty thousand, including Sabbeans, Quorali, Vizals, and Estraloths. They wait for war on the ancient battlefields of The Acheron Plane; not a day passes without additional forces joining them.

"Grave news indeed," I declared. "If they grow daily, we best hasten the day of battle."

I returned my eyes to Evagrios, "My friend, it is not fit that The Absoluçion should ride into war brooding. Speak to your men and command their heads to lift. The sullen soul will not stand steady and strong on the battlefield. Suffering under the weight of loss, their hearts are too heavy. The fractured earth of Moranor is already weak; gravity will force your soldiers down to their grave."

Evagrios, his countenance drawn and despairing, countered, "If your eyes had beheld devastation as ours have these past days, you would know you ask the impossible. How can I command my men to lift their heads when my own is bent on death and destruction? I am weighed down by thousands of images. Zombies haunt every moment of my waking and my sleeping."

"I saw the desolation of Sorrentas, and felt your pain whilst the smile sat easy on your face." I empathised. "Evagrios, you are the leader of The Absoluçion, and leaders do not have the privilege of being disheartened. Lose heart, and you lose courage; lose courage and you will hinder the battle. As will your men, for they mirror your attitude."

"My smile has flown from me like a bird in a storm. It is lost and I know not where to find it."

"You may not be able to fabricate the superficial smile, but there is a deeper joy within. Search beyond your grief, for in the depths of your being lies dormant the Seed of Life, the joy and strength of the Universe. Here take my hand and you will see."

Seeking to help him find that which had come to me, I un-gloved my hand and took a firm grip upon his. Nothing happened at first; but warmth gradually gathered like a whirling wheel in my spirit, eventually reaching the extremities of my body. I willed that power to flow from me into Evagrios. Light, that heavenly Song that had been transmitted to me, I transmuted into him. His body shook as the lightnings flashed in his soul and the volcano began her eruption. First, the bursting cap, flushing from him the outer layers of pain and suffering with tears and rending moans, then finally joy. No flippant amusement of the shallow man, but the steady flow of a deep river, the laughter of The Eternal, and strength with it.

Many would think we were too few as we rode toward the mark, a hundred against more than fifty thousand; but I counted on this: we were One. The multitude surrounding Rochel on the Acheron Plane may outnumber us many times over, but we were the Monolith, the Rock, they were a mere mound of pebbles, the rabble, a puerile pile of rubble. A promise also was buoying my heart; Uriel had said to look for him on the Fields of Death.

CHAPTER

The Golden Sea

Abandonment! The thought sets terror into the heart of all mankind, and with good reason, there is no greater dread than being one of the forsaken. Yet such fear rises from the depths of the soul deformed, and surfaces solely because we are hitherto unformed. In that fear we are held to ransom by all our earthly attachments, human and inhuman, the multiplicity of entanglements that provide our ego with its sense of existence. When someone, or something is taken from us we feel torn asunder, and then we fall apart. We are like the fallen egg that can't be put back together again, for our shell is shattered into the multitudinous fragments of a fractured existence. However, this existence is false! It is the mirrored Labyrinth of *Mutatis Mutandis*; a pretentious subsistence.

We abhor the notion of abandonment. Yet, I was learning abandonment is the one thing necessary; it is the sacrifice The Father of all requires. Sacrifice is the making of a man! Only in abandonment, only in forgetting about myself, will he, he who I am called to be, he who is truly I, finally materialise.

Confronting Chemosh's dungeon, Eden's beatification, Ruâch's molten wave, these catastrophic leaps of monumental development are pivotal; but no less important is the daily grind. Every movement and thought contains the utmost consequence. In each and every moment, I am in the making and must abandon myself to the will of The One.

"Something on your mind?" Suso enquired, and gaining no immediate response, he sought again, and again, until he drew me out of my musings.

"Another dream has come to me," I confessed.

"Tell me, if you will: Your dreams have weight enough for more than one to bear."

"Very well, then listen to this: A dark hand, shaped like a claw, stretched over the horizon intent on obtaining that which this mortal world cannot offer. Yearning for the invisible, lust drove it beyond all natural barriers, until it grasped the untouchable. It disappeared momentarily, creating a black cavity in the universe, a vortex, into which the dark hand was sucked and all materiality with it, including light of sun, moon, and star."

"That's a disturbing dream if ever I've heard." Suso pondered, "Was that all?"

"No, there was more, but the end I cannot recall."

Our destination was approaching. According to Nassûr, only a few days ride lay between us and Rochel's hive. Food, thanks to Montobora's pantry, exchanged upon promise of our departure, was adequate. But Nassûr advised us to turn from the Acheron Road in order to circumvent any ambush Rochel may have set. Our detour bore us away from the river, and consequently, our expected source of water. For a number of days, we endured thirst without complaint; but it was with great relief that we came across the seldom seen *Waters Illuminæ*, or The Golden Sea of Illumination.

Illuminæ's waters lay nestled in a rise surrounded by trees in constant bloom. Pure white blossom drifted in the breeze, giving a panoramic impression of freshly fallen snow. Aromatic honey wafted upon the air, and the soft drone of bees was music in our ears. We all, horse and man together, drank deeply from the brook that flowed in several directions through the grove. Thereafter, travel weary bodies relaxed upon the soft carpet of white petals. This would be our company's final opportunity for respite before battle, so I let them have as much as they required. Rest would have been welcome to my limbs also, but first I determined to investigate the copse.

Suso accompanied me as past three lines of trees we encountered an ancient arch upon which was etched an invitation for all to enter and quench their thirst. I gestured toward the inscription, but Suso had not the vision to see that it read:

> *Drink and be Satisfied*
> *But best be Wise*
> *To Imbibe these Waters*
> *Is to Drink through your Eyes*

Soft sunlight filtered through the snowy canopy and pursued us as we descended timeworn steps into the hollow. The interior of the well was lined with ancient stones reaching toward the ceiling; they were intricately carved and gilded with gold. Between each step, worlds unfolded, one into another, until direct light was replaced by an amber glow which danced upon the golden walls. Stepping onto the base of the staircase was a step into silence, reminiscent of Ruâch's underground forge. There, a pool mirrored perfectly the interior of that sacred place. The water shone like liquid gold. It seemed but a pond when I first looked but it slowly swelled into a limitless golden sea. I was shocked to see reflecting back at me not he whom I expected but a somewhat different me than the one my eyes had previously viewed. My reflection had become more than I remembered: the face looking back at me was simultaneously younger yet stronger.

Suso's thirst intensified with each step toward the water. Without hesitation he reached into the satiating liquid and drank in delight. When the ripples settled, my face was no longer reflected. In its place I beheld a star that shone bright, but which then turned black to the core. It rose and assumed authority over a second star more glorious. Behind the black star was the claw from my dream reaching across land and sea. It extended authority, until a vortex formed into which was drawn all materiality, including the heavenly lights. From within the vortex a loud voice declared, "The time has come! This is the end! Mark your name on the field of the Immortals!" The vision faded into my golden reflection.

"That's what I call a drink!" Suso exclaimed, wiping the back of his hand across his mouth, "Never in this entire world have I tasted the like. Eden alone has water to compare."

I laughed. He had observed nothing of the well vision, but it was not for Suso to see. He possessed other gifts and the waters satisfied those completely.

Returning to our comrades, we found them refreshed, restored, and ready. Suso and I, having drunk from the well, felt fully replenished for the pending battle. We left Illuminæ's waters brimming with anticipation; the kind that only comes through strong camaraderie, shared purpose, and the undergirding of great joy.

As we descended the white hill, the bee's harmonics faded into the background; but then returned, disturbed. The bothered drone grew louder, and agitation with it. Suddenly a creature flew at us from the sky. It was a wyvern, and it was not alone: A dark cloud of winged beasts swarmed over us.

Under attack, we continued advancing; our shield-maidens keeping the evil at bay with their arrows. Soon others, larger and more menacing, railed; wolf and warg and wyrm. Though the horses were fearful, they did not falter, and we resisted the savage attack without a single one of us falling.

"Rochel seeks to hinder us," I claimed. "Proof that whilst possessing weight of numbers, nonetheless, he waits in fear."

Sorties from those damnable beasts dogged the final leg of our journey.

CHAPTER 36

The Fields of Death

Under the pallid eye of a sun that fought with ebbing strength to guide our way, we arrived at last on the Acheron Plains. We had entered the dunkelflaute. The air was thin; we were suspended in its silent breath. Tension stretched its talons toward us. An occasional roar spilled over the horizon and rolled across the plain. Standing soundless before the distant storm, we observed black fires peppering the distance, choking the air with the industry of war.

Evagrios could remain silent no longer, "So, at last you have arrived at your destiny, my lord," he chirped. "How goes it with you now?"

"Here is not my destiny, Evagrios. I have given this place little thought since entering the *Acies Mentis*. Were Rochel not between us and Avalon, we would simply march on. Since he stands in our way, we must march through him. This day is his choice; not mine. It will be his doom. Nevertheless, he shall have opportunity to recant and rescind his death wish."

"Really?" Suso queried.

"Soon the two of us shall ride and offer Rochel salvation."

"No! No! No!" Evagrios spluttered his objection. "You cannot! Bestowing clemency for treachery? Never! Surely you can see this is unwise, no? Charity for the destroyer? For the scoundrel who devastated you and all you loved? This is not reasonable! It is not right! It is unjust! Give him what he deserves: sever his head with one strike of your sword!"

"No, my friend; I brought that harm upon myself. Had I been more of a man, more like my father, he would not have usurped the throne. In weakness and ignorance, I handed it to him. My arrogance and pride robbed me, and all of Moranor."

"What about the massacre at Moranor? Surely, he must pay for his crimes against our land and people?"

"He has done more than massacre, Evagrios, he has depleted the very substance of this country. Pay for his crimes, he will. Nobody gets away with anything! You'll soon see." I had more to say but thought it best to hold my tongue. Too many words do too little good. Action will provide the proof Evagrios requires. "Enough talk. We must prepare for battle."

Evagrios found it difficult to zip his lips and rest content, "But did you not say you are offering Rochel the opportunity to recant?"

"Offer it, we shall, but he will not receive it. Fear drives him to war; fear, with a good dose of malice, and, above all, pride. And pride permits no pardon that precludes power."

The sun waned into ambiguity shortly before reaching her apex. We lit a singular fire, a large blazer that stimulated centrality to our camp. Around its crackling flame, our dour group gathered. Those with a long history of war rested. Others, unable to sleep, busied themselves sharpening swords, checking, and rechecking equipment, encouraging one another, praying.

Anxiety threatened to rob many of this opportunity, a brief moment wherein life's appreciation is acute simply because we faced our own mortality. So, I encouraged those at hand, "Hold your nerve. We have been brought here, not to die, but to truly live. Stay close to me, follow my command, and you will see what power lies in strength and integrity. Do not fear what they fear! Should death make its stride toward you, be sure to die well, in the knowledge you live forever, crowned in memory, song, and the Great Beyond."

Mist swallowed the vacant space between earth and heaven; we did not see the sun set nor rise; no bird greeted the dawn, no splashing fish, or rustling rabbit. One lone sound was heard, and felt, drum thumping. Suso and I were riding toward enemy lines. Midpoint we stopped, and hallowed the ground, salvaging it for the good of Moranor.

"Do you feel it?" Suso whispered, "Do you sense yesteryear's battle continues on this theatre? That we are walking where friction and ferocity have been silently waiting for this very hour? It is poised to break upon us!"

Though nature had been busy erasing the carnage that previously bludgeoned this country, the chaos of ancient hostility was evident. I could see beneath the surface, red as lava, a seething subterranean anger ready to assault the land of the living.

"Yes Suso," I agreed, "And today, with Omnipotent help, we will bring war to its end."

Fleetingly, the mist opened like drawn curtains. A broken sun sat astride the hills; the great eye pierced through the vermillion ambience with a single shaft of light. The pounding drums were silenced by the sun's wand. Suso and I filled our hearts with the light. Alas, it was but a moment before the curtains closed and the drums recommenced their dreadful dirge.

At the rear of the enemy's ranks a large canopy had been constructed toward which we advanced, intent on parley. An innumerable force had congregated; staring, wondering, tawdry spectators of our audacious approach. As they glared the crowd divided, and seven warhorses marched to meet us. Five wore the red serpent. Another was shrouded in a dressing of burgundy, a living mummy covered in blood-soaked raiment. The central figure, I surmised, was Rochel. Over his armour he wore a mantle, all white with a golden cross; his shield bore the same, Moranor's coat of arms.

Rochel met us under a kismet of his own making. I calmed the sudden rush of blood that would have me run him through. As grace was given me, so I was determined it should be ministered to him. He lifted his visor, and I saw the long-forgotten sneer, "Dorranor, what brings you out of your dungeon?" His voice oozed through the slime of his corruption. "And, where is your precious Uriel? *That Nervenarzt!* How do you hope to keep your mind together without his psycho-babble?" His fury was foaming, "He has deluded your juvenile mind with thoughts of grandeur. To presume I will relinquish the title, privilege, and honour that is rightfully mine, is madness." A psychopathic cackle escaped his mouth.

Rochel continued with protracted taunts and mockery. Through it all I remained silent, vigilant, waiting for him to run out of words. I waited long. Those with nothing to say habitually speak too much about everything that amounts to nothing. Eventually, I had to break in on the diatribe, "I seek nothing from you Rochel, for you have nothing to give. In fact, I am the one with something to offer."

Confusion wrestled cunning on the field of Rochel's face, "What could you possibly offer me, Dorranor?"

"Your soul, Rochel. What could be more valuable than your soul?!"

"So, you have become a priest since dillydallying in Chemosh's courts," he snarled contemptuously. "How magnanimous of you to suggest you can barter with something that is mine."

"A priest? Yes, of sorts, for I offer you forgiveness, Rochel. Accept it, and stand judgement for your crimes. This is your only hope."

The offer of forgiveness tore at Rochel's pride, "A king commits no crime. He is law!"

"If you were king that might be true, but you have never been a king. You cannot be what you are not. Title, is meaningless. Being, is everything!" As sharp as an arrow, my words tore through his armour and pierced Rochel's heart. "Meet me alone on the open field when the sun is high and let The Most-High decide. He will be your judge."

Rochel's discomfort was palpable, escalating toward a state of alarm. Those with him were mirroring his discomposure, "You are a tragic vexation!" he blurted, malice and fear uniting in a cauldron of childish rage, "You have always been the bane of my existence. Be gone, or I'll pin your pathetic hide to the earth and leave you for the vultures."

I felt pity for him, "Is that your decision?"

"Dorranor! You are the hero of your own comedy, or should we call it a tragedy. You see before you an incalculable force; and you come to me with words and a rabble. You are a charade, a caricature, a sham. The least you could have done was to bring an army worthy of a contest."

"Do not take comfort in the size of your battalion, Rochel. Everything requiring numbers for significance, is by that very fact insignificant. One, is the only prerequisite necessary to set heaven and earth alight. It is the individual who garners the attention of The One."

Rochel's sneer smirked derisively, "Surely you don't think that you can achieve anything today except feed yourselves to the wolves. You will die, you and yours. You'll go down without honour or remembrance."

"I have died already!" I countered. "I have experienced Chemosh's chamber. There is nothing you could do to me that has not been done before. Now, I wish to address your army."

Rochel's jaw dropped. He attempted to stop me but I had bandied with him enough. He'd had his chance. I raised my hand, and, as happened with the Nephilim outside Nemesis' cavern, quite unaccountably, and to everyone's astonishment, I disarmed him and fixed him like a petrified tree.

Leaving Rochel and the others glued to their place, Suso and I sought Moranor's banner. Once found, I addressed those gathered under the golden cross, "Men of Moranor." (Among them I recognised Luga and Arrelay; Luga, looking worse for wear; the Nephilim made him pay for losing me in The Metaxu.) "You assemble here in the name of tyranny; I come in the name of The Most-High. Reconsider your ways and heed my call, for this day the kingdom will change hands: Of this you can be assured! Loyalty has merit, but not for its own sake. Genuine loyalty is aligned with truth and love. If Rochel owns your heart, then you will suffer with him. But, for those who remember a better way, the way of my father, Celorn the Sublime, I offer the opportunity to reforge your allegiance where it belongs, with The Living Light. Today, I call for you to enter the battle with me."

Silence was screaming; a clash of wills ensuing; a battle of authority, competing for the heart and mind of Moranor.

"Well, what of it?" I demanded.

The air was being stretched. Finally, one man, standing tall and broad, released himself from the invisible serpent that coiled around everyone's throat, and turning, he pushed his way through the crowd, back to where Moranor's banner stood. He dislodged it from the ground and bore the standard high. No word passed his lips, but his action spoke into the hearts of Moranor's warriors. With steely eyes and his jaw set like flint, he strode past me, past Rochel, and continued through the fields toward our camp on the other side of the Plane. Others followed.

Again, I raised my voice, "Any here belonging to the free-world, any who love life, I adjure you to return home or you will never see it again." None moved: Breaking the tyrant's spell is easier said than done.

"Then I have nothing to offer you," I continued, "By tomorrow you will rot in the caverns of the damned."

When I unmuzzled Rochel, his veins were bulging and his eyes flaring. The Serpanta found themselves in a similar state for they reflected their master's nature. There was no point in talking further, his heart was unyielding. Having rejected his opportunity to repent, he was irredeemably blind and could see nothing but blood.

Suso and I gave them our backs as we rode away to the sound of Rochel screaming madness and promising slaughter. We caught up with the defectors, nearly a thousand of them.

"I recognise you," Suso declared as we drew alongside the one holding Moranor's banner, "you are Eckhart, military commander of Moranor."

"*Former* military commander." Eckhart replied.

"Seems so." Suso laughed.

"No!" I exclaimed. "You have lost nothing in coming with us, except the favour of Rochel."

"Rochel's favour, I never sought; I serve Moranor alone, and would serve her still. In all my days under Rochel's rule I saw nothing but Moranor's dismantling, and the grief that accompanied the process. Seeing your return, hearing your words, live or die, I can do nothing but offer you my sword."

"Well said," Suso harmonised, "I am Suso, and this is…"

"I am the fallen." I interrupted, before Suso could say more. "I am honoured, Eckhart, to have you join us."

CHAPTER 37

The Beginning of The End

There was barely enough time for us to assemble ranks before Rochel struck. He launched neither arrow, sword, javelin, or any weapon remotely conventional, but evil craft was measured against us, a wave of darkness, a shockwave aimed low, knocking no less than a hundred to the ground.

"Stay alert, and stay on your feet." I commanded. "Let nothing of the enemy catch you unawares. Stand, I tell you. Stand, and stand strong."

Another sinister jolt thumped into us bearing more power but less effect.

I marshalled the army, "You are the free! Yours is the victory! You are the lightning of *The Mysterium Magnum*! You are the thunderbolt of His wrath! You are the straight arrow in His golden bow! Do not be intimidated by the size of the horde across the plain. Do not be impressed by that which matters little; what matters here is *will*! They have many wills. That is their undoing. Our enemy is a fractured bone awaiting the telling blow. When it comes, he will shatter." I called Eckhart to join Suso and myself. He came bearing Moranor's banner, and I continued my charge, "Today we assemble under the banner of The Cross! Today, we welcome death! Yes, consider yourselves dead: Dead to all, but alive to The One! One mind! One heart! One will! Like the angels above! The kingdom is at stake, and we shall take it by force."

A third wave screamed toward us, the scream of universal agony. Some in our contingent betrayed elements of fear. Trepidation remained for as long as the agonising cry reverberated. I traced its trajectory: Through the mist, standing on the opposing side of the plane, I saw the mummy, brazen and bloodied, with her drones, the Nephilim, busy at work.

"That one in the middle," Cassian explained, "the one in red, who has just been joined by the Nephilim, that is the one affecting the air. Every time those beastly hands are raised, we feel the effect."

"That is the Chimaera." Eckhart affirmed.

"That can't be!" I declared. "The Chimaera was destroyed when my father rescued Verona from Nemesis' lair."

"Yes, but its black seed remained in the hearts and minds of The Seven who were slain. After retrieving the Nephilim from Chemosh's tomb, Rochel took that seed, and through sorcery she was reborn. She is still young, and, as yet, has not recovered all her power; otherwise, there would be none who could withstand her."

"Then we should not let her grow any older." Suso enjoined, sword in hand.

I unsheathed Aléthéa, her light illuminated the mist, and she filled the air with her clarion call; she thrilled at the battle pending, for light shines brightest in darkness; and she thrilled all those who were on the side of Light. "Listen, listen to her sing!" I shouted to those under my command, "Fill your hearts with the Eternal Song, and let your swords join Aléthéa in rapturous symphony."

With our faces shining in her light, we launched our assault; three hundred horses, the others on foot. Sure, and deliberate, we advanced; the steady potency of footmen behind a shield of horse and rider; horse and rider the spearhead of the infantry's might. Our advance preceded and precipitated the enemy's, whose drums bellowed like apocalyptic thunder on that apocalyptic morning. En-mass they became an advancing wall that spanned the deathly plane. Fear saturated warheads continued their bludgeoning assault; an invisible procession threatening to segregate those to whom fear can cling from those who brush it aside as one does a fly. I observed each attack and issued warning and encouragement as was necessary. Were Uriel with us, he would not have allowed the Chimaera's continual intimidation; I looked for him, but he was not there. What I could see, however, what at all times I could behold, was the seething lava of subterranean anger rippling beneath the surface of the Acheron Plane; and I could feel its predicating doom.

Strategizing to exploit any chink in Rochel's armour, our strength lay in speed and accuracy: We would sever the enemy's outer pinions, thus creating a wound through which we could inject a virus of doubt. Toward the selected target we flew, stretching and forming the shape of an arrowhead, riders to the front and riders to the side. Nearing the point of contact, we feigned left and veered right, closing in upon their flank, the juncture, where Easterling mercenaries marched beside vagrant Quorali.

Suso, Cassian, Eckhart, Evagrios, and I tipped the arrow. The speed and valour of my warrior-friends induced holy horror in the spines of those before us. Fear bulged through their eyes, and white terror was the canvas for the paint on their faces. We scythed right through them and out the other side, placing us at the rear of a hundred thousand men. They were slow to react. We swooped along their right flank cutting a swath through the Easterlings who could barely fight, but scattered like rabbits into the forest.

Whether through self-preservation or bitter rivalry, the Quorali appeared reluctant to assist their Easterling cohorts. This proved to be their own undoing, for our next thrust was aimed at them.

Thus, the battle was initially waged. We were fleet of foot, too fast for the fat lumbering hand of the giant against which we fought. Our achievements injected confusion and panic into the hearts of any we threatened. Those who live by the sword shall die by it; those who live by fear shall perish in it.

Trumpets brought the giant's march to a halt. We moved away from its clumsy fingers intending to regroup in a safe location and measure the situation before executing our next stroke. But no such refuge existed. Rochel haply sacrificed the lives of Quorali, Easterling, and Vandari to gain himself position on both sides of the plain. Our rising confidence reached an abrupt end as the enemy arched around us; their pincer broken only by The Acheron's broad flow. We could hear the impetuous giant bellowing a ludicrous guffaw as we assessed the development and discovered, to our utter peril, that the villain had set his trap and we had flown directly into it.

Fear wrestled with the hearts of my men; not a few were falling to the Chimaeras' escalating terrorism. "Look up, each and every one of you," I called, seeking to clear heads and free hearts from the enemy's supernatural onslaught. "Fear is an illusion; there is nothing in it except what it can find in you. Keep your focus. Do not take your eyes off The Banner, set your eyes upon The Cross! And remember, for such a time as this you were born. Come we shall fight with our backs to the river."

We jockeyed to the water's edge, and turned to face the enemy. Just then a roar went up from the opposing crowd. It was the premature shout of victory. They were looking downriver to where sails stretched in a lifting breeze; the armada was parading Saba's black colours. The situation appeared grim, we were totally enveloped; and it was fast growing worse, for beyond Saba's ships, beyond what others could see, I saw a second armada bearing toward us.

CHAPTER 38

Revelation and Resurrection

Rochel seemed content to keep us cornered, subjecting us to various intimidations, taunting us across the embattled plain. The red plague persisted in her sophistry, propelling carnage. Other catapults joined hers, flinging fireballs through the air, as well as the bodies of fallen soldiers, ours and their own. None of this was performed systematically; Rochel was biding his time, waiting for Saba's armada, closer by the minute, to arrive.

In the course of this torturous interlude, it also pleased Rochel to entertain himself with a little sport. He spoke at length with the Chimaera, his hands compulsively folding over and over each other as though lending some spell to her armoury. In response, the Chimaera did not so much disappear as dissolve. Her blood-soaked bandages flowed to the floor and lay temporarily empty and dormant before they began twitching and convulsing, contorting and distorting, then morphing and assuming animalistic contours, all hunched and predatorial.

"My lord." Suso interrupted. "You've been wounded!"

"That can't be; I was not struck."

"But your leg bleeds." Suso directed my attention to an old wound; a tear in my leg was seeping bloody puss.

Out of the crouched creature an ominous sound evolved, a gurgle that bubbled and boiled into a terrible wail. Men, near and far, shielded their ears. That sound triggered vague memories; identification, however, was evasive, until unfolding itself, the animal's proportions and manner of movement ushered recognition to the fore. It was the shadow-beast from hell, materialised in all its deliberate, imposing, swollen arrogance: Body of a lion, head like a wolf, black and skulking from its shoulders; its hair spiked along a raking backbone, dark stripes ran like ribs along its flanks, yellow fangs protruded from a salivating jaw, the eyes were slant and evil, their colour parading between red and orange.

Unable to contain her blood-lust the marish shadow rushed upon those nearby, flaying and thrashing a dozen or so Vandari in a brief psychotic frenzy. Those poor pathetic plebs had been packed together so tight they stood no chance of escaping the beast's wrath, whose rage brooked no dissimilation between good and evil but feasted upon the terror manifest in those who came under her attention; she destroyed for destructions sake. The Vandari erupted in pyroclastic panic. More were torn asunder; more than a few were consumed. Rochel stood on the side-lines laughing, the raking cackle of the lunatic despot.

The carnage did not fail to make its impression upon our army; many turned pale, some found themselves shaking uncontrollably; not a few wept. Suso moved to confront the beast, but I stopped him. "No, Suso, I would not risk your life at the hands of the Chimaera. I know what to do."

I dismounted my horse, immediately feeling weakness in my bloodied calf. 'I have bled and limped enough from this,' I thought, 'and I'll no longer be subject to its power.' So, I withdrew Aléthea and aimed her sharp tip toward the weeping wound. Suso looked to stop me but I remained steadfast. "It is right that I do this. If I bleed, it will be from light and not shadow."

Aléthea's blade sank deeper and deeper into the wound, taking almost the full length of the shaft before I could feel she had reached the end of darkness and was touching living tissue. Thick puss bubbled and frothed from the injury, oozing out to form a black icy pool on the ground at my feet. It flowed until no poison remained. For a moment, a current of fresh blood trickled down my leg. Then, Aléthéa grew warm in my hand, and her brilliance cauterised the lesion.

I made for the beast that was brooding its way toward us. The Chimaera accelerated, disgorging a limb here and a body there as she hastened her approach. I was running, my sword high and ready to strike. Just as we were about to clash, I saw her hesitate and take a more defensive stance; whereupon I stayed my ground and challenged, "So, the evil queen returns. You know who it is you face? My father, Celorn the Sublime, ruined you on the Forgotten Mountain. It was he who sent you to *nihil*, and to there you shall return."

Intense rage wailed her response. With Aléthéa gleaming in my hands the beast commenced a circular prowl, an enclosing standoff that locked in long enough for Saba to arrive. Rochel's camp renewed their vitriolic hurrah, which had me briefly glancing to see if my men were under siege. The slight distraction was all the beast required. Suddenly, I was the one besieged. In one fell move Aléthéa was jolted from my grasp and my shoulders were pinned under paw. Those slant orange eyes turned red and rolled in demonic delight, cold pride revelling in her prize, the seed of her nemesis. Saliva joined with the rain drizzling over me. A rancid reek was in my face, the weight of death upon my body. Struggling proved pointless, the beast was too heavy. Unable to move, my doom had come. Then, why inside did something leap? Why was a secret sensation filling me with concentrated celebration? In the inner sanctum, where the song discovers it's melody, I surged.

As I lay in this counterpoint state, subject to death but thrilling with life, the monster opened its mouth and revealed an appalling abyss, the doorway into Hades. She raised her head, eyes lusting and rolling, and teeth ready to plunge. I braced but felt no impact, no pain. Instead, abruptly, and remarkably, I perceived fear and fever, and I saw light and flame. Screaming terror, the beast let go; and there, above my body, she reduced to her former form, now robed in fire. Suddenly, in a flash of light, she was not. Then, I saw why; for beside me was Uriel, and with him Ungründ, the unicorn, smoke wafting from his flaring nostrils. Rochel observed it all in stunned perplexity.

Joy burst through my skin, "Uriel!"

"Come quickly," he called, "before Rochel breaks out of his suspense and comes after you."

Sheathing Aléthéa, I adjured, "But Saba's ships have reached us; my men will need our help."

"Saba has not come to fight, but flee, he does, from the Valoria who pursue him up the Acheron. Now, hurry!"

I followed Uriel to where thickets merged into the foothills of Ravens Forest. There, surrounded by shrubs, I saw a heap of rocks carefully mounted one upon another.

"This mound was built by the Valoria after the Dark War." Uriel informed. "These stones honour the valiant whose lives were lost in the war against treason. At a time when you cared not for yourself or for those under your care, they gave themselves for you. Restless, they lie beneath the Fields of Death, awaiting the end when the ancient prophecy declares their rising."

"Is this the hour when you will bring them from the grave?" I interjected with unrestrained eagerness.

"It is not for me to release them." Uriel replied. "With you they descended; it is for you to raise them up."

I was taken aback, "How can *I* raise the dead?"

"You must place your name into the deathly field. It is in your name, the name given you by *The Mysterium Tremendum*, that they will rise to follow the true king."

"My name remains a mystery; though I have tried, I cannot recall it."

"Your name was chosen from the foundations of the world, but you never really knew it, you never achieved its grandeur." Uriel's voice was grave, "However, since your rebirth your true nature has evolved, you have become worthy of your name. Hurry! Remove the memorials; they have served their purpose. Into the earth beneath you must plunge Aléthéa and release The Immortals."

One by one I lifted the stones and passed them to Uriel who placed them in a semi-circle such that the opening gaped riverward. "Were these stones not placed so," he explained, "the dead would rise all over Moranor."

With the last memorial removed, a hollow was revealed in which lay a single white stone, its surface polished, and upon it a name was inscribed which filled me with wonder.

Uriel smiled, "The white stone was placed there by me on the day you were chained to Saba's tower. It bears your name, the name you have searched so hard to find. Now do with it what you must."

From deep within, from the secret and arcane juncture where true life lies hidden, I called upon the dead to return to life, for those who fell in honour to rise in greater honour. Thrusting Aléthéa into the earthen cavity, I spoke that name written in stone. In that name I called for the sleepers to arise and awaited the consequences.

Scanning the Acheron Plane, I observed the battle. In the background the Valoria were running Saba's armada into shallow waters. Before them, Suso and the valiant were holding their ground, tight against the river. But superimposed upon that scene I saw the boiling turbid fury, a swirling, surging, elemental rage, screaming, rushing, threatening, and flooding.

Rochel remained convinced that the sheer size of his army ensured victory; and it looked that way, until, with a seismic shift, the ground began to change at an elemental level. That rain sodden earth melted like lava, pulsing and bubbling and glowing with unearthly vibrancy. With a groan the surface burst, and from it emerged the faithful warriors of Moranor, The Valiant, The Resurrected. They knew what to do. Upon the evil foe they flew, the return of the dead, now living. The corrupt looked behind to see the avalanche descending upon them; their faces pale; they swallowed rage and vomited fear. The aggressor regressed and The Resurrected prevailed.

CHAPTER

The Sounds of Silence

Accumulated activity, great and small, gallant and common melded together to form one great Act, the kind of union that transforms the world. Of heroic deeds performed that day there'll be no end of telling, nor will songs enough be sung to honour those who, withstanding overwhelming odds and nefarious fury, won through to ultimate victory. Here it will suffice to mention but a few:

The courage of Urshûah, Kareah, and Serene, who together kept the demonised hordes at bay, conjuring a force field through which few could penetrate. In their hands the simple became sublime, as their bows and arrows were turned into weapons of mass destruction. A frenetic blur, they put so many darts through Rochel's front line that the enemy faltered and vacillated whilst The Resurrected emerged. Never a shaft from bowstring sped so fast through thin air as the arrows of the shield-maidens of Avignón.

The self-effacing challenge of Rôbard, Olmănn, and Böhemen of The Resurrected, who stood toe to toe with three Nephilim; who considered not their lives though newly restored from the sub-terrain, but with enduring force and daring, took on those feared for their speed and cunning, even slaying one of the dark masters. Whereupon another two lords of the damned amalgamated and conjured a spectre with many hands and legs and eyes and teeth, emanating fear and poison and wasting disease. It towered above them and put on such deceit that it drove them to near insanity. Still the three fought the colossus without fear or fatigue, until the end was come and all was consumed.

Suso, whose chivalry is unquestioned, waded deep into the enemy's lines, and measuring himself a quadrant, called for all who dared to cross the line and try their hand against him. En-mass they swarmed until he was lost from sight. Yet out of that mass he clambered and rose above them. His sword appeared, as observers remarked, to be ten swords or even twenty, for that blade in his hand became a silver haze. A mountain was formed that day on the Plains of Acheron, made from the carcasses of the enemy slain by Anselm, son of Aneurin.

Then there was Uriel, who located himself wherever things waxed worst, who shone in the darkness, who's voice sang loud and strong. Leaping on Ungründ's back, into the tumult he weighed with staff and sword and word of power, withstanding the titans drawn up by Rochel from the nether regions. Uriel defeated them and sent them back to the caves from whence they came, bound in iron and the embarrassing robes of their miserable trouncing.

Also, at a time when the enemy's confidence was gathering, when their momentum seemed to be building, from out of the blue rode Luhrs leading fifty of Montabora's mounted warriors. Having ridden three days and nights, they struck the enemy so hard that thousands leaped into the Acheron and drowned.

Finally, the indescribable, the end of war and of this world: Over many months, power from the sun had been waning, light and warmth diminishing. Come the day of battle, a pallid sickly atmosphere prevailed, a perpetual twilight; the time between times had arrived. The failing glow of that errant orb tended to work its way into the bones of those who love the Light, affecting a depression that threatened us with discouragement. This effect was intensified when the sun passed noon and its trajectory tracked downward. The receding light was affecting the battle. That was when I called, under Uriel's approving eye, for the sun to reverse the fall and return to his peak. At once the daystar retreated several paces and remained at its apex for as long as was necessary.

Rochel, observing the enduring noon, grieved over the length of day, and became more anxious when he saw the battle shifting in our favour. In dread desperation he turned, and with two Nephilim beside looked to flee. But I was not about to let him get away. His evil, I would not endure another day. It all ends here! So, I mounted my horse and raced after him. Suso followed suit. We accosted the unholy trinity at the edge of Raven Forest and plied Rochel with questions regarding his intentions.

"Do not think for one minute that I am fleeing the battle, Dorranor," he answered. "The world remains in my hands; it was never yours, nor shall it ever be. Your war bandying may give you a tiny thrill, but I am about to strip you of all possible self-congratulation."

Rochel turned to his spectral partners, and they turned on us. Aléthéa was quick in my hands, her light blinding fierce. Suso found himself duelling with Vennar; their powerful blows tolled across the plain.

The Nephilim fought with hand and word, each blow delivering the severity of annihilation. In grace, Aléthéa parried the assault, but Suso had no such weapon of light, his sole illumination being that which radiates from within. So, it was that I dealt more speedily with my challenge, and, venturing to help Suso, he, with some desperation, claimed Vennar for himself and suggested I would best serve the world by attending to the viper, Rochel; so, I attended him.

Not far from where Suso and I contested the Nephilim, I saw Rochel kneeling at the rise from whence I received my name. Through the memorial stones I approached and heard him chanting in the murky language of the underworld. I had not heard words like that since suffering in Chemosh's dungeon. He faced me, forced a wicked sneer, and then thrust his hand into the earthen cleft, "Do you think it is for Moranor that I fight, Dorranor?" he crowed. "You are a greater fool now than when I consigned your insignificance to Saba's tower." Rochel's hatred crackled to the surface and burst into anxious, sycophantic laughter.

Resuming the ill-omened incantation, the mystery of his evil was revealed to me, for at that moment in a parallel world I saw the hand of evil reaching from graven dimensions, stretching from darkness to light. Having devised a way to penetrate the impenetrable, Chemosh was assuming the throne of paradise and entering Eden. Suddenly a light, brighter than a thousand suns, burst around us, and all the sounds in the universe were sucked into terrible silence. Then there was nothing, nothing but awe and potentiality, for this world had reached its end - and another was beginning.

CHAPTER 40

Uriel's Song

Uriel stood and commanded everyone's attention, "It is my greatest pleasure to bring you a new song I've called: *"Fostering the Noble Man:"*

Daring or bravado by no means convey
The evil day, dim venture's description
Rather those lower forms of knowledge
Presumption, assumption
Are more accurate expression
Of evil's intention
Of Chemosh's carriage
When foolishly seeking to bind in marriage
Damnation with perfection
The Abyss with The Mountain
He, thrusting his vaporous appendage
Into the Living Fountain,
The legendry kingdom, the glorious Eden;
Anti-matter clawing for all that matters,

The insubstantial grasping substance actual.
And therein perforating the world unfallen
Seeking glory for his own.
Instead, he ruined his ruinous throne.

For the end came suddenly,
In a flash of perpetuity;
From east to west the lightening strobed;
Into a vortex all did implode;
When Eden caught his hand; And, pulling him in,
He crashed with all that belonged to him.
Great Silence consuming his clamour
The Light terrorizing terror
And the world that waxed senility;
The world we knew succumbed to gravity;
Was sucked and swallowed into Terrible Beauty.

Beyond the Light, beyond the Song,
Did pour the world, its rights and wrong.
By Magical Mystery all did stew,
Before transforming, regurged, renewed.
In reversed implosion,
Explosion's cost;
In the Great Revision,
Nought was lost.
Save evil's personality.
When wrong was made right
On that Silent Night
By Evil's proud audacity.

Through that nest absorbing all,
The good returning through narrow door.
But evil hordes at once consumed,
And what was left of them assumed
Their rightful place bound in doom,
Together with all those deviant devout
Who choose to suffer everlasting drought.

But two were saved by deeds of valour,
As can happen where 'ere there's honour.
For when the implosion first was felt
Instead of sending Vennar to hell,
As they were streaming from the land
Suso took hold his brother's hand.

Into the narrow portal entered,
Suso's will, firm and centred,
Saw Vennar grow awf'ly thin,
Stripped of arrogance, emptied him.
Till there was nothing left to hide…
Barely there, stretched thin as air,
Just a seed there did reside;

His own true soul, weak and empty,
The stretch, the strain, so greatly pained
That Vennar pled, "Show some mercy…
I adjure thee to release me - into the night."
But love held on with all his might,
And with him travailed through pain and woe,

'Til out the other side he flowed.
Bearing Vennar in his arms, though maimed;
Sanity reformed; his name remained
Among the restored of Moranor
Gathered in the Mighty Hall.

Then there came the kingly act:
Forgiveness' flow in virtuous charity;
For Rochel's hand was surely trapped,
And from it there'd be no deliv'ry.
Nought could describe the burning horror,
For the fate of Chemosh, Rochel did mirror;
Aligned in life and united in terror.

The risen king with Aléthéa's light
Wished to relieve Rochel his plight;
Bargained repentance for recantation
To spare him of terrible damnation.

The dark prince refused, preferring his curse
None other would have joined debate;
But the king still pressed for the reverse,
Delivering Rochel redemption's fate.

Aléthéa's blade sliced him asunder,
Severing his arm below the shoulder...
"Better The Kingdom without your hand,
Than wallowing in hell as a fallen soldier."

URIEL'S SONG

The vortex round and round them sped,
'Till Rochel's screams in silence dread,
And there before the Judgement Throne,
The king requested in merciful tone
Rochel's survival no matter the form;
Life for life he would atone.

So, the false prince reluctantly returned,
Chemosh's tortured child deformed:
A miserable creature as yet unborn.
And though he thinks it not,
His anguish one day will be forgot.
Till then blessing he bears so troubled…
To sit with the king is to be ennobled.

Now it came upon return
Of the fallen king unfallen,
Peace complete and justice firm
Would irradiate the kingdom.
The curse was lifted from the land,
From mountain and valley and sinking sand;
Healing imparted with earth's salvation,
Arriving only with destruction
Of all that was destructive,
Of every thing that was corrupted.

Avalon waiting in golden splendour
For the king to bring the waking sleepers,
The Resurrected accorded to ancient lore

> *Entered the streets of Moranor,*
> *Greeted by salubrious roar;*
> *Fulfilling the prophecy, that ancient scroll,*
> *Except for one thing that must be told,*
> *By a new name the king is called,*
> *For the heavens and the earth do now behold,*
> *That he is called Dorranor no more,*
> *But Bhrmmn the Brave, Bhrmmn the Bold.*

The song was applauded by the assembly; all except Rochel, who remained dis-armed, cowering in the corner of the feasting hall. My continual hope is for his restoration. Uriel says it is a fool's hope. Perhaps it is a mad savage's hope. Nevertheless, it is mine. I could not let my adversary go into eternity without tasting as much grace from my table as has been presented to me by The One who each day grants me a feast in the presence of my enemy. Though Rochel receives it as contempt and mockery, though he hates and reviles every morsel offering, his torment is self-originating and self-deprecating.

As Uriel settled beside me, I probed, "That was a grand song, but I missed hearing the name."

"How could you miss the name? It is your name. I am sure nobody else did. Is it my enunciation you are questioning, or perhaps my projection?"

"Neither! No doubt it is my hearing that is questionable."

"You have that right." Uriel said laughing. "You know who you are well enough, and your guests have drunk to your honour; So, you have no need of repetition. Unless, of course, you like the sound of it so much that you must tire me out with the uttering."

I had not forgotten my name, but I was still growing into it. Quite simply, I didn't like the fact that I missed hearing it when it was spoken. So, I held my expression.

"Well, if I must," Uriel relented, "it is *Brrrmn*."

"Sorry, I still did not catch it."

"More likely it did not catch you." Uriel answered, his tone becoming grave. "Open your ears, sir. Wake up *Brrmmn! Brrrsssmn, wake up!*"

From the other side of the table Eden chimed in, turning the repetition into a veritable chorus, "*Brmmn! Brrssmmn! Brrrssssmmn!*" That was when I felt someone shaking me.

CHAPTER 41

The Final Awakening

"Brosnan! Brosnan! Wake up! *Brosnan!*"

Must there be no end to these confounded awakenings? For the name repeated, though at first, I could not bear, eventually bore through the veil of my subconscious and transported me from one world to another. Dreams rushed into filtered light, until, opening my eyes, I beheld Evelyn kneeling over me, her face lined with irresistible concern. Sir Justice Thorogood stood behind her, quite unfazed, "Oh my boy, you have returned, and none too soon. Your poor wife was getting quite desperate for your welfare. Wanted to call the doctor, she did! Wanted to take you to hospital, she did! Such a fluster you have caused her. But now she can see that I was right, and you are all right after all." He was positively beaming.

Evelyn's apprehension remained; holding my hand, stroking my face, and taking little comfort from the professor's words.

"I do not think you will profit any more from those extravaganzas," he continued, "The job is complete, more or less, now that you have got it all together: body, soul, and spirit. And a fine job has been done at that. There can be no discounting the workings of *The Mysterium Tremendum*. When The Good Lord decides to work on us, He leaves nothing undone."

Customarily, I emerged from these catatonic states completely alert, and this occasion was no different. The Old Girl was chiming 10pm. "Well, if that wasn't the most vivid dream of all. Sorry to have fallen asleep on you, it's no comment on the value or interest of your company. I simply haven't had enough sleep lately. I must be more tired than I realised."

"Nonsense, Brosnan!" Evelyn said, her voice alarmed and indignant. "You have not been asleep; you have had another of your spells."

"That can't be!" I answered. "I always return from those occasions drawing a blank; those periods are a complete mystery. This time I woke, bringing the dream with me. I have vivid recollection of battle and treachery, and nobility. And, Sir Justice, I believe you were in it, but you had a different name, and you were a bard or something more."

"The Lady Evelyn is right, to a point, Brosnan," Thorogood affirmed, "It was no mere dream. It was and is Reality. You could call it *a real dream*. I will explain it all to you in good time. For now, there is somewhere we must go."

"Where exactly would that be?" Evelyn inquired, her sense of offence rising defiantly.

"Oh, just over to the University. We must get there soon. We're due there now, in fact."

"I do not feel up to it." Evelyn sighed, her tone and press of my hand urged my assent. Yet, I could not resist the pull of Justice Thorogood's words. I squeezed Evelyn's hand and was up on my feet.

"My lady, are you sure you won't join us?" Justice entreated. "Granted, it is unusual to go wandering the neighbourhood at this hour, but you will find the adventure most invigorating."

"No, I do not want to go on any late-night adventure. I have had enough escapades already this evening. I am going to retire." Evelyn's voice was a tense fusion of disapproval and anxiety. "Brosnan!" She looked piercingly into my eyes. (How I loved her in that moment.) "You should see Sir Justice to the door and bid him goodnight."

I kissed Evelyn and held her in firm embrace, trying my best to be reassuring, "Really darling, you should come with us," I advanced hopefully, "I doubt if you'll sleep until we return anyway. Surely you are curious? Surely you want to see where all this is heading? Haven't you been hounding me to move beyond the study?"

Leaving Evelyn was not easy; she was so apprehensive, so fragile; but I would make it up to her. In fact, I was now convinced that only in the completion and realisation of these recent anomalies, only through their revelation, interrogation, and integration would I be able to truly and selflessly be the man I ought to be; and the husband she needed me to be.

Once the door closed behind us, I headed for the car. Thorogood looked up at the sky and with a gleam in his eye suggested, "I could do with a walk, if you don't mind? The snow has stopped and the sky is clear. What better time to walk. Cars are much too hasty for my liking."

The faculty at St. Simone was a community. We walked the laneway past their homes, beneath streetlights that illuminated the recent snowfall and filled the night with an amber hue, the ambience hinting that we lived on the doorstep of enchantment.

The cobblestones of Sunnyvale Drive were slippery underfoot. A figure loomed in the distance barking a raking cough. Furtively and nervously, he came, slipping and sliding toward us. That slippery fellow turned into the image of Ramose. Under normal circumstances I would have attempted avoidance, not for any reason other than sheer distrust, plus a smidge of contempt. This occasion was different: Overriding my suspicion was a compulsion to engage him with nothing less than a shake of the hand. As Ramose approached, it became obvious that he was the one who was struggling with our chance encounter; he, it was, who was searching for an avenue of escape; but there were no avenues leading from Sunnyvale Drive.

He met my outstretched hand with a customary sneer; but before those jarring, gyrating noises all came flooding to the fore, Sir Justice quickly dispersed any possible conversation, "With such a cough, you ought to be off home, quick smart." In spite of his curiosity concerning our late-night stroll, Ramose reluctantly obeyed and slipped into the night at a brisk pace.

Something struck me in those few seconds with Evelyn's cousin, and I drew it to Justice' attention, "That was the strangest thing: When I shook Ramose' hand, his sleeve crimped up his arm. I could be wrong, but I'm sure he has a tattoo. Not that I saw much, but I'd swear he was painted with anarchy and mayhem, like Picasso's Guernica, and entwining it all, the figure of a snake."

"You are not wrong," Thorogood confirmed. "Ramose has many branches, many fingers in many worlds. He is a coadjutor in the underworld, belonging to a secretive sect which operates under the name *Nephilim*. Thousands of years old it is, and full of every kind of evil. That serpentine tattoo is their insignia."

Sir Justice spoke broadly concerning their history. By the time he finished we were deep inside St. Simone, descending to parts of the building I had never previously ventured, to a place Justice Thorogood called The Hegemonicon, what St. Augustine and Gregory the Great called The Acies Mentis, in English, "The Eye of the Spirit".

"Here we are." Sir Justice Thorogood's face was a mixture of pleasure and purpose. Before us, two heavy doors hinged upon a massive archway. "Inside, should you choose to enter, lies discovery; discovery and fulfilment. Therein your calling will be unveiled. Behind this door is the chamber of the Valoria. Tonight, I have gathered several of its knights to meet with you. You may recognise one or two from your alumni. They're inside, waiting and praying, praying and waiting," he paused, and seemed to grow taller before concluding emphatically, "for you!" Then he laughed, a short, but heartfelt, laugh.

I was perplexed, "For me? Why for me?"

"Because, Brosnan, you are chosen, and you are charged to lead the Valoria."

I stood like a dumbstruck ox. I had stepped back in time, and from my dreams the past had come to me.

"You see, Brosnan, you have arrived at the place where all that matters has melded into one; rare enough in the human scheme of things, and on its own, that would not be enough for me to bring you here this evening. You were chosen to be here. This very moment was predetermined for you millennia ago because you possess those quintessential qualities that qualify you to lead such an order; you have the calling on your life, and you have insight, you can see what needs to be. Calling and seeing! It's as simple as that!"

"*Calling*? True, strange and wonderful things have been happening recently; but a *calling*?" I was intrigued by the word.

"They have not had a leader for over three hundred years. I have been looking after things for them in the interim. Only a seer can lead the Valoria. You are a seer, as you have recently discovered; and you are chosen to be their leader. You are called, if you heed the voice that is calling."

It was all so intense that I deflected, "You have been leading the Valoria for three hundred years?"

"No, I am not a member of the Valoria. I come and go as I wish, as necessity demands."

I should have felt incredulous, hesitant, even doubtful; instead, I was young again, out on an adventure, a wonderful exciting venture, beyond anything I dreamed life would hold. "Allow me one question." I was speaking rather rapidly, a little too excitedly for my own liking. "I will go through that door, but I sense that once I do, there is no turning back. What assurance can you give me that I am, as you say, *called*? For I do feel something has been calling to me, or rather, urging me, something beyond this world and yet very much part of my world. Yet I have no aspirations to lead anything; let alone some extraordinary league. Surely some assurance is required?"

Thorogood's jaw squared up and he stood tall, "It is sufficient that I say you have it; but those inside that door, they will confirm it. Search your heart and you will see it is so! Do not remain a stranger to the truths that lie therein. I urge you to take up my charge, for to whom much is given, much is required."

We entered the room and in the following hours my past, present, and future fused into one.

That night saw the end of my catatonia. Upon returning home, and after much apprehension and the most intense scrutiny, Evelyn grew in her appreciation of my awakening. Sir Justice didn't revisit with an explanation of my archaic dream, he didn't need to; the peace and gratitude, insight and enlightenment, were self-evident. No longer the desperate man, gone was the distant husband, no more the fractured existence gaining identity from career and association, success or failure; now there remained love and peace, courage and truth.

PARALLEL WORLDS

Peace, love, truth, and courage
For these the worlds of man aspire
Enduring hope of age new-born
When bearing all we are entire

But prior to the dawning
Fallen worlds collide
Existence disharmonious
Undone, unfree and uninspired
Chained and simultaneously
Restless until they and we
Are forged in one identity

This, once discerned we do distress
Until in our hearts they are possessed
Dissatisfaction again returning
Deducing in the striving
Perfection lies beyond the grasping
Beyond our making
Discovering in truth the certainty
It is they affecting the possessing
Yet commanding no ability
Bereft of essential efficacy
To create such Perfect Harmony

And too noble by far is man
To be owned by any thing
No trinket, concept, ideal, or happening
Only in Faultless Relationship
With Perfect Personality
Can we be both bound and free
To be owned and to own
All that forms True Unity
To return us to Integrity
Forging faith
Imparting strength
Infusing man with dignity

www.ingramcontent.com/pod-product-compliance
Lightning Source LLC
Chambersburg PA
CBHW032111090426
42743CB00007B/312